REEF CORAL
Identification

FLORIDA CARIBBEAN BAHAMAS
Including Marine Plants

PAUL HUMANN
NED DELOACH

NEW WORLD PUBLICATIONS, INC.
Jacksonville, Florida USA

Acknowledgements

This book was the result of considerable encouragement, help, and advice from many friends and acquaintances. It became a much larger undertaking and involved many more people than ever expected. The authors wish to express their sincere gratitude to everyone involved.

Long time friend Adrien Briggs, and the entire staff at Sunset House, Grand Cayman helped make our photographic trip to the islands most successful. Fellow underwater photographer Cathy Church and her staff kept our cameras working and provided important daily developing service. Diving companions Sol Fiser and Mike Bacon were indispensable assistants in finding many of the cryptic corals. Wonderful friends, John and Marion Bacon gave generously of their time, assistance, and boat, helping me photograph corals of East Florida. Captain Dan Morrison, Captain Julie Jordan and Jason Wesley of the Aggressor Fleet offered valuable assistance in finding uncommon species. Mark Ulmann's knowledge of northeast Florida's reefs was most valuable. Peter Hull and Gary Gilliland with Mote Marine Laboratory, in Sarasota, Florida, expedited our locating and photographing several species unique to West Florida. Taxonomic updates for the 3rd edition were provided by Ann Budd, Steve Cairns, Judith Lang, Ken Marks, Mark Vermeij and Ernesto Weil.

PHOTO CREDITS

Mike Bacon, 211t&b, 218bl, 219tr, 223ml; *Dr. Andrew Bruckner,* 229br, 231m&b, 233m&b, 235tm&b, 236b, 237tm&b, 238b, 239tm&b, 240m, 241m&b, 242m&b, 243br, 245b, 246b, 247tm&b, 250b, 251m&b, 253m, 255t&m, 257b, 258b, 259t; *Jeri Clark,* 136ml; *Ned DeLoach,* 78m, 79t, 82b, 83m&b, 85t,m&b, 91b, 108m, 109t&m, 210ml, 243bl, 244m&b, 245t&m, 249t, 263t&b, 264br, 265tm&b, 266tm&b, 267t&b; *Guillermo Diaz-Pulido,* 119b; *Alexa Eliott,* 102br; *Nicole Fogarty,* 103m&bl; *Ken Marks,* 16bl&r, 17t, 18bl&r, 20m&b, 21m&bl&br, 22ml&r&bl&r, 23tm&b, 103t, 128m&bl, 130ml, 133m, 134bl&br, 135b, 141b, 142m, 143m&b, 144bl, 145b, 148ml, 150br, 151b, 174mr, 175ml; *Ken Nedimyer,* 21t, 102ml&r; *Doug Perrine,* 264t&bl; *Scott Porter,* 185m; *Mark Vermeij,* 115t; *Dr. Ernesto Weil,* 117b, 121b, 149b, 151t&m; *Raphael Ritson-Williams,* 103br; *Aletta Yniguez,* 102bl; the remaining pictures were taken by *Paul Humann.*

CREDITS

Editor: Ken Marks
Photography Editor: Eric Riesch
Art Director: Michael O'Connell
Print Consultant: D'Print Pte. Ltd., Singapore
First Edition, 1992; Second Edition, 2002; Third Edition, 2013
First Printing 2013, Second Printing 2015, Third Printing 2019.
ISBN 978-1-878348-54-8

Published and Distributed by New World Publications, Inc., 1861 Cornell Road, Jacksonville, FL 32207, Phone (904) 737-6558, www.fishid.com, orders@fishid.com

Scientific Acknowledgements

Special thanks must be given to the scientists who gave freely of their time, advice and knowledge. Each is a preeminent authority in their respective field, and without their most generous assistance this book could have never been published. Every attempt was made to keep the text and identifications accurate. Where errors exist, they are the authors' sole responsibility.

David Ballantine, PhD, Department of Marine Sciences, University of Puerto Rico, offered valuable advice and help with the identification of algae.

Frederick Bayer, PhD (deceased), longtime curator at the Smithsonian National Museum of Natural History, Washington, D.C.

Andrew Bruckner, PhD, Chief Scientist with the Living Oceans Foundation, is a coral reef ecologist specializing in coral diseases and predation. He compiled the text and provide photographic documentation for Appendix II: Coral Health and Mortality, which he updated for the 3rd edition. Because of the state of decline of many corals this is an important reference for monitoring the health of Tropical Western Atlantic coral reefs.

Ann F. Budd, PhD, Department of Geoscience, University of Iowa, Iowa City, IA, assisted with general taxonomy for the 3rd edition.

Stephen Cairns, PhD, Smithsonian National Museum of Natural History, Washington, D.C., acted as the primary advisor for stony corals, providing assistance with each of the three editions. He substantiated the identifications of many species from collected samples of photographed specimens. These specimens are currently part of the permanent National Collection. The samples' "USNM" identification numbers have been placed next to the appropriate photographs in the text.

Dale Calder, PhD, Royal Ontario Museum, Toronto, Ontario, assisted with the identification of fire and lace corals.

Deborah Danaher, MS, reviewed the stony coral text and helped compile Appendix III: The Reproduction and Growth of Stony Corals.

Douglas Fenner, PhD, Department of Marine & Wildlife Resources, American Samoa, a coral reef monitoring ecologist helped locate a number of uncommon species and helped establish visual identification clues for *Agaricia* species.

Nicole D. Fogarty, PhD, Nova Southeastern University Oceanographic Center, Hollywood, Florida, assisted with Fused Staghorn, *Acropora prolifera*.

Walter Goldberg, PhD, Emeritus Professor of Biological Sciences, Florida International University, Miami, Florida, deserves special mention for his work as the principal scientific advisor for the 1st edition. His help with the collection of several species of unidentified octocorallian gorgonians is greatly appreciated.

Walter Japp, PhD, Emeritus Professor at the College of Marine Science, University of South Florida, St. Petersburg, Florida, examined and identified several collected specimens of stony corals.

Judith Lang, PhD, Atlantic & Gulf Rapid Reef Assessment Program, acted as the primary advisor for scientific name changes of stony corals and provided general information for the 3rd edition.

Dennis Opresko, PhD, Research Associate at the Smithsonian National Museum of Natural History, Washington, D.C., and world's expert on black corals helped with the identification of many obscure species.

Scott Porter, EcoLogic Environmental Consulting, serves as an investigative environmental marine biologist.

Ernesto Weil, PhD, Professor of Coral Reef Biology, Ecology and Systematics, University of Puerto Rico, suggested many meaningful changes and provided important photographs.

Jennifer Wheaton, PhD, Florida Marine Research Institute, St. Petersburg, Florida, acted as the primary advisor for octocorallians. Her field knowledge was invaluable in establishing visual identification keys for numerous species.

Vassil Zlatarski, PhD, an independent coral researcher, made many helpful suggestions and provided details about Honeycomb Plate Coral, *Porites colonensis*.

About the Authors

Paul Humann & Ned DeLoach

To find Paul Humann at his south Florida home, you have to cut through his dining room, which is lined with primitive art from jungle civilizations around the world. The large family room, no less impressively decorated, showcases fish, turtle and whale carvings – each the creation of island hands. A splendid collection of his favorite Galapagos wildlife prints covers the left wall; a dozen fiercely proud New Guinea tribesmen stare down from their tack-sharp portraits on the wall just to the right of the back door. Outside, a wooden deck, perpetually shaded by a towering mango tree, curves to the right under spreading limbs dripping with fern and orchid baskets, passes through a jungle of Australia tree ferns and bromeliads, and ends abruptly before a nondescript aluminum storm door that opens into the unkempt garage/office of an extremely busy man.

Whenever Paul has been in the States during the past 30 years, he has spent most of his time here. Early mornings to late evenings find him wedged in a pre-1970 K-Mart swivel chair that sits hopelessly trapped by fallen reams of drafts, correspondence and scientific publications before the tireless glow of a computer screen. Steam from a stained mug filled with strong Ecuadorian brew spirals up from the clutter. On the unfinished plyboard table to his left are two color-corrected slide viewing boxes, spread with an ocean of blue transparencies, illuminating book shelves packed with a well-used marine life library. From a nail hangs a cheaply framed Juris Doctor degree – a relic from an almost forgotten time. The remainder of the 10 X 29 foot concrete floor supports cheap, metal shelving piled with various office supplies, darkroom equipment and an unplanned museum of underwater photography equipment. A few dust covered pieces date from mid-century – the embryonic era of underwater exploration. The only order found anywhere occurs behind the thick, double doors of a large fire safe where carefully labeled and neatly stacked transparency storage cases hold treasures from 40 years of bountiful underwater hunting with a camera.

Though Paul's photographic search for marine species started in the 1960's, it really began in earnest in 1971 when he left a successful law practice in his hometown Wichita, Kansas to buy and captain the now legendary *Cayman Diver:* the Caribbean's first successful live-aboard diving cruiser. This bold move offered the unique opportunity to dive daily with the exotic creatures of the Caribbean reef. Paul sold the yacht in 1979, gaining even more freedom to travel, write and explore the world's coral reefs.

Hard work, continuous study and the courage to follow his dream, have led to the publication of 14 books, numerous magazine articles and a three volume *Reef Set*. Paul's pioneering efforts in marine life identification have required much more than capturing each species on film.

Collection, preservation and shipment of photographed specimens to scientific mentors around the world were required to establish identifications for hundreds of species.

Even with all his accomplishments, Paul has no intention of resting on past achievements. He continues to write and teach about marine life and gather information and photographs for future editions of the *Reef Set*. He does, however, plan to spend less time in his office and more time where he loves to be – traveling the world.

After finishing a degree in education in 1967 Ned DeLoach moved from his childhood home in west Texas to Florida so that he would be able to do what he loves best – dive. In 1971 he completed his first diving guide to the state, *Diving Guide to Underwater Florida,* which was released in its 11th edition in 2004. In the mid-1970s Ned and Paul co-edited *Ocean Realm* magazine. It was during this period that the idea of a marine life identification series designed for divers was born. In 1989, the 1st edition of *Reef Fish Identification* was published by New World Publications, Inc., their jointly owned marine life education publishing house. Beginning in 1995 Ned and his wife Anna spent five consecutive summers in Bimini, Bahamas researching fish behavior for the book *Reef Fish Behavior* written in collaboration with Paul and published in 2000. Ned and Anna live in Jacksonville, Florida.

Authors' Note

Corals flourish in warm, clear, shallow seas. Along the Florida Keys' Atlantic fringe, throughout the Bahamas Island chain, and spreading south and west across the tropical waters of the Caribbean Sea, great coral reefs proliferate. Towering sea-sculptures adorned with waving gardens of flexible coral fans, whips and plumes provide sanctuary to one of the Earth's most diverse and visually stunning ecosystems.

It has only been with our recent ability to freely explore this dramatic underwater wilderness that we are beginning to unravel its complex nature. Even with limited data, it is readily apparent that environmental changes both natural and manmade have had a harsh impact on coral habitats. Coastal development, oil spills, overharvesting, groundings, climate change, ocean acidification, El Niño, algal blooms and storms–the list of culprits is long. Our lack of knowledge, however, is the reef's greatest threat.

An ancient Chinese proverb states: THE BEGINNING OF WISDOM IS GETTING THINGS BY THEIR RIGHT NAME. A single, healthy reef section may consist of over 50 coral species, but only a few divers are able to identify even the most common corals. The ability to recognize individual life forms on the reef is the critical distinction between an underwater sightseer and the underwater naturalist.

The guardianship of the world's coral gardens should, by right, be led by the recreational diving community. For decades bird watchers have been accumulating a wealth of data by monitoring bird populations. Their enjoyable pastime has produced an invaluable resource for their environmental concerns. Comparable information about the reef's inhabitants remains unavailable even for areas that are visited by thousands of divers each year. It seems sensible that recreational divers should make a similar commitment to marine life by taking an active role monitoring our coral reefs.

Reef Coral Identification is the first comprehensive photographic guide for the visual identification of corals and marine plants that inhabit the Florida, Caribbean and Bahamian waters. It is designed to help underwater naturalists, as well as scientists, distinguish the many species of coral, algae and coral diseases encountered while exploring the reefs. *Reef Coral Identification, 3rd edition,* is the third book of the three-volume *Reef Set* that includes *Reef Fish Identification, 4th edition,* and *Reef Creature Identification, 3rd edition.*

Contents

Twelve Identification Groups
Common & Proper Phylum Names

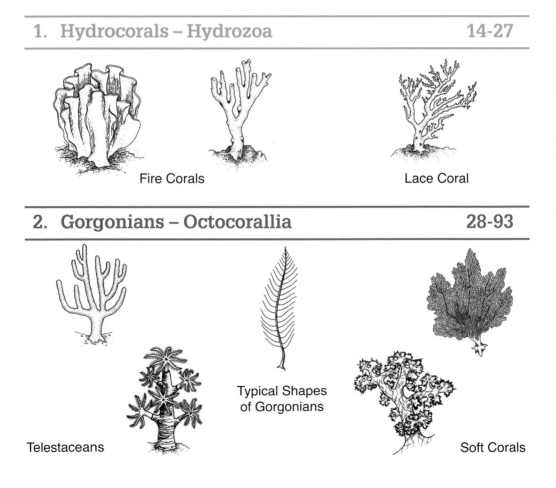

1. Hydrocorals – Hydrozoa   14-27

Fire Corals   Lace Coral

2. Gorgonians – Octocorallia   28-93

Telestaceans   Typical Shapes
                    of Gorgonians   Soft Corals

3. Stony Corals – Hexacorallia 94-195

Encrusting, Mound &
Boulder Corals

Branching & Pillar Corals

Brain Corals

Fleshy Corals

Leaf, Plate & Sheet Corals

Flower & Cup Corals

4. Black Corals – Antipatharia 196-207

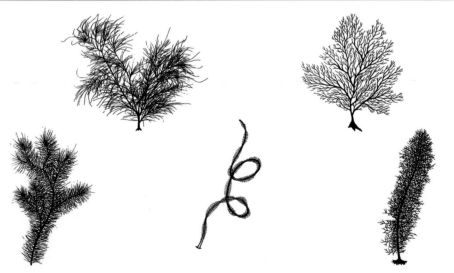

Typical Shapes of Black Corals

Overview

Corals are tiny animals that generally group together by the thousands, forming colonies that attach to hard surfaces of the sea floor. By drawing calcium carbonate from seawater they build skeletal structures in an infinite variety of shapes and sizes. Those species known as reef building corals, produce massive skeletons that collectively form the limestone framework of tropical reefs. Throughout the ages a vast array of animals and plants have become associated with coral reefs, creating some of our earth's most fascinating, complex and biologically diverse ecosystems.

All corals are members of the Animal Kingdom and classified in Phylum Cnidaria (Nigh-DARE-ee-uh/ L. a nettle [formerly known as Phylum Coelenterata/L. open gut]). They are often mistaken for plants because of their attachment to the substrate, apparent lack of independent movement and superficial resemblance to flora. In fact, corals were classified as plants until 1753, when French biologist J.A. de Peysonell, making a study in the Western Atlantic, concluded they were animals. Although corals are the best known cnidarians, the phylum also includes several other well-known groups including hydroids, jellyfish, and anemones.

Cnidarians have a simple anatomy consisting of a cup-shaped body, with a single, central opening that is encircled by tentacles. This opening functions both as a mouth and anus. Most phylum members attach their bodies to the substrate; in this form they are known as polyps. Polyps can live singly, such as most anemones, or they can reproduce asexually to form ever expanding colonies, which is typical of most corals. Noncolonial, unattached, free swimming members of the phylum are known as medusa or jellyfish. A unique characteristic shared by virtually all cnidarians is the presence of numerous stinging capsules, called nematocysts or cnidae, which is the origin of the phylum's Latin name. These minute capsules, located primarily on the tentacles, are used for both capturing prey and defense. With the exception of fire corals, the stings of most corals have no harmful effect on divers.

For coral reefs to develop, the delicate polyps must flourish. This requires several critical environmental factors, including: water temperature, movement, salinity, clarity, and a firm base for attachment. Water temperature must generally remain between 70 and 85 degrees Fahrenheit for the reef building colonies to grow. Species can survive below or above these points, but do not grow at a rate sufficient to construct reefs. Water movement sustains life by refreshing the supply of planktonic food and oxygen. Water clarity is also important. It allows the passage of light, essential for the growth of single-celled plants, called zooxanthellae (zo-zan-THEL-ee), that grow within the coral polyps' tissue. Zooxanthellae play a vital role in the polyps' ability to produce calcium carbonate for their skeletons. Reduced clarity, caused by settling silt particles, limits the polyps' ability to feed by literally choking them. Even under ideal conditions coral growth is slow, measuring less than an inch each year for most species.

In addition to the reef building corals this volume also includes the cnidarians commonly known as fire corals, lace corals, gorgonians (sometimes called soft corals) and black corals. All other cnidarians are identified in the companion volume, *Reef Creature Identification*. Marine flowering plants and algae play a vital role in the reef's ecosystems and are included in Appendix I. Many of these species, known as coralline algae, also employ calcium carbonate to support their structure. In this way they contribute substantially to the reef building process by filling voids and actually cementing the reef's framework together. Appendix II – *Coral Health and Mortality*, compiled by Dr. Andrew Bruckner, a timely addition to the 2nd edition because of the proliferation in the past decades of diseases affecting corals throughout the region, has been significantly updated and expanded. In many areas the majority of shallow-water branching coral gardens have been lost to disease infections for yet undetermined reasons. Hopefully, this review will serve as a standard resource for groups and individuals monitoring the spread and affects of coral diseases so that we can better understand the causes and dynamics of this daunting phenomenon. Appendix III – *The Reproduction and Growth of Stony Corals* present a delightful pictorial essay of one of natures most majestic procreations: the annual mass spawning of corals.

Types of Coral Reefs, Structures and Terms

The basic types of coral reefs are generally defined by their overall structure and the geological conditions under which they evolved. These distinctions are sometimes obscure because of overlapping stages in the continuum of their development. Most marine scientists agree that there are at least three basic types of coral reefs and possibly as many as five. In broad terms, the reef types may be described as follows:

Fringing Reefs grow out from the shore or are separated by a shallow lagoon. They generally parallel the coastline and at their shallowest often break or nearly reach the water's surface. They are common around most Caribbean and Bahamian islands, but are virtually absent along both Florida coasts and the Florida Keys. Geologically they are considered to be the youngest type of reef.

Barrier Reefs generally grow parallel to a coastline, but are separated by extensive distance and a relatively deep lagoon. The distance may vary from about one mile to 25 miles or more and the lagoon often exceeds 60 feet in depth. At their shallowest they often break or nearly reach the water's surface, forming a "barrier" to navigation. The outer edge of a barrier reef drops from the island platform or continental shelf into very deep water. The best example in the Western Hemisphere is the world's second longest, skirting the small Central American country of Belize. Typically, fringing reefs change to barrier reefs when their associated land mass undergoes a slow geological sinking.

Atolls are open sea reefs that form rings, ovals or horseshoe-shapes around a shallow lagoon. Occasionally small coral islands that may support vegetation form as a part of the ring. On the outside the fore reef drops into deep water. Atolls are generally found in the tropical Pacific where large geological plates supporting volcanic peaks gradually sink. Fringing reefs first form around the volcanic islands. As the plate sinks, the reefs become more distant from the land and grow upward, forming barrier reefs. The final stage of an atoll's development occurs when the volcanic island is completely submerged, leaving the lagoon in its place. There are a few atolls in the Western Atlantic, but they were not formed from submerging volcanos as in the Pacific. The best known are Lighthouse, Glovers' and Turneffe off Belize, Chinchirro off Yucatan and Hogsty in the Bahamas.

Bank Reefs are open sea reefs, without a central lagoon, surrounded by deep water and miles from any land mass. The Great Bahama Bank, Ten Mile Banks off Grand Cayman, and Serranilla Bank and Misteriosa Bank located in the Northwest Caribbean are well-known examples. Some scientists also describe the reefs off the Florida Keys as bank reefs, while others consider them as a combination of bank and barrier.

Patch Reefs are small, isolated reef areas that grow up from the open bottom of the island platform or continental shelf. They generally occur between the fringing reefs and barrier reefs, if present. A patch reef may vary in size from a small house to an area that could cover several city blocks. Depths also vary greatly, but the reef's crest rarely breaks the surface.

Coral Heads are similar to patch reefs, but smaller in size. They are primarily formed by a single coral colony, such as a huge brain or star coral, but may include several smaller colonies of the same or different species.

Reef Crest is the top of a reef system.

Back Reef is the area behind fringing reefs, usually protected, calm and often containing a mosaic of shallow coral heads, patch reefs and turtle grass.

Lagoon is a relatively shallow, calm, protected area behind a fringing or barrier reef. It often includes great expanses of sand flats and grass beds and occasional coral heads.

Fore Reef is the area on the seaward side of any reef, but refers primarily to the portions that project into deeper water.

Tongue & Groove are long ridges separated by valleys of sand that generally run toward the direction of the prevailing swells. They often occur in shallow water near the reef crests, but may also be found on the fore reef. The ridges are also termed spurs or buttresses. The valleys are also called sand channels, sand chutes, and, if narrow with high, steep sides, canyons.

Walls are underwater cliffs that drop at or near a 90 degree angle. They are often associated with the outer limits of an island platform or continental shelf.

Wall Lips are ridges that often form and run along the upper edge of a wall. The ridge can be slight or over 20 to 30 feet in height.

How to Use This Book

The animals in Phylum Cnidaria are classified further by scientists into class, order, family, genus and species. Similar appearing Cnidarians, commonly recognized by the public as a group, such as fire corals, stony corals, black corals, etc., usually fall completely within one of the lower classifications. These **Commonly Recognized Groups** are important reference keys for using this text. The predominant anatomical features that distinguish each of the twelve groups included are summarized in their corresponding Identification Group introductions. Stony corals, because of their large number, are further divided into six structural/appearance groups. All groups are also listed with a visual reference diagram under their associated group in the contents pages, in the quick reference index on the inside back cover, at the top of the left page where their members are described in the text, and in bold type next to the identification photograph. It is important, as a first step in coral identification, to become familiar with these groups and their locations within the text.

Names

Information about each species begins with the animal's common name (that used by the general public). Using common names for identification of corals by scientists is impractical because several species are known by more than one name. For example, Grooved Brain Coral, *Diploria labyrinthiformis,* is also commonly known as Depressed Brain Coral, Labyrinthine Brain Coral and just plain Brain Coral. The common names used in this text are based on previously published names. If more than one name has been published, the one most commonly used or the name which best incorporates an anatomical feature that would help the layman remember and recognize the species was selected. Previously published common names are listed in a "NOTE" at the end of the text describing each species. Several species included have never had a common name published. In these instances, a name was selected that describes a distinctive feature that can be used for visual identification. It is hoped that the common names used in this text will become standardized so future confusion will be eliminated. In this book common species names are capitalized to help set them apart, although this practice is not considered grammatically correct.

Below the common name, in italics, is the two-part scientific name. The first word (always capitalized) is the genus. The genus name is given to a group of animals with very similar physiological characteristics. The second word (never capitalized) is species. A species includes only animals that are sexually compatible and produce fertile offspring. Occasionally "sp." appears in the place of a species name, this means the species is not known. If a "n." proceeds the "sp." it means it is a new, scientifically undescribed species. Continuing below genus and species, in descending order, is a list of classification categories to which the genus and species belong. This scientific nomenclature, rooted in Latin (L.) and Greek (Gr.) is used by scientists throughout the world.

Size

The average size range of the species divers are most likely to observe. Occasionally, the diameter of coral cups, branches, etc. is also given if this information may be useful in visual identification.

Depth

The reported depth range in scientific literature, although species are occasionally found outside these limits. The depths at which a species is most commonly found are given in HABITAT & BEHAVIOR. Depths below the recommended recreational safe diving limit of 130 feet are given only as a matter of scientific interest. Species that live exclusively below 130 feet are not included.

Visual ID

Colors, markings, and anatomical differences that distinguish the species from similar appearing species. In most cases, these features are readily apparent to divers, but occasionally they are quite subtle. Generally the coral's colonial structure is described first, followed by distinguishing characteristics, and finally colors. If the colonial structure of the species is fragile, this information is also included in this section.

Abundance & Distribution

Abundance refers to a diver's likelihood of observing a species in its normal habitat and depth range on any given dive. This is not necessarily indicative of the actual populations. Definitions are as follows:

Abundant - At least several sightings can be expected on nearly every dive.

Common - Sightings are frequent, but not necessarily on every dive.

Occasional - Sightings are not unusual, but not on a regular basis.

Uncommon - Sightings are unusual.

Rare - Sightings are exceptional.

Distribution describes where the species may be found geographically within the range of this book. The Turks and Caicos Islands are included as an extension of the Bahamas Island chain. Described species may also be found in areas such as Bermuda and Brazil, but no attempt has been made to include this specific information in every identification, although additional data has occasionally been included. In many instances the extent of a species' geographical range is not yet known; consequently, species may occasionally be found in areas not listed. If sightings are made that do not correspond with the geographic information provided, the publisher is interested in obtaining details for updating future editions.

Habitat & Behavior

Habitat is the type of underwater terrain where a particular species is likely to be found. Habitats frequented by divers, such as natural and artificial reefs, adjacent areas of sand and rubble, seagrass beds and walls are emphasized.

Behavior is the animal's normal activities that can be observed by a diver and used in identification.

Effect On Divers

If a species is known to have a negative effect on divers, it is listed. The agent of the injury, how it might occur, symptoms, and recommended treatment are included where appropriate.

Similar Species

Occasionally there are similar appearing species that are not pictured. Generally they are corals and marine plants that for one reason or another are rarely observed. Characteristics and information are given that identify and distinguish them from the species pictured.

Note

Additional information that may help in the visual identification process such as: recent changes in classification and nomenclature, other common names also used for the same species, or details relating to the method used to identify the photographed specimen. Several photographed specimens are now part of the National Collection at the Smithsonian. Their catalog numbers (USNM) appear next to the specimen's photograph.

Class Hydrozoa
(High-druh-ZO-uh / Gr. water animal)
Hydrocorals

Hydrocorals are hydroid colonies that secrete hard, calcareous skeletons. They are often thought to be stony corals, but the resemblance is superficial. There are two types, fire and lace corals.

Fire Corals

ORDER: Anthoathecata (An-thuh-A-thee-cot-a/ L. flower and unsheathed)
SUBORDER: Capitata (Cap-ih-TA-ta / L. head-bearing)
FAMILY: Milleporidae (Mill-LEE-pore-ih-dee / L. thousand pores)

Fire coral, or stinging coral, as species in the family are sometimes called, often produces a painful burning sensation when touched by bare skin. The pain is usually short-lived and neither severe or dangerous. For a few sensitive individuals, however, it can cause redness, welts and a rash that can last for several days. This reaction is caused by unusually powerful **batteries of stinging nematocysts** on the tentacles of the tiny polyps.

In the event of a sting never rub the affected area or wash with fresh water or soap. Both actions can cause untriggered nematocysts to discharge. Saturating the affected area with vinegar immobilizes unspent nematocysts; a sprinkling of meat tenderizer may also help alleviate the symptoms.

The hard, calcareous skeleton of fire coral appears relatively smooth. Close observation, however, reveals a fuzzy covering which is actually the colony's tiny, hair-like polyps extending through thousands of **pin-sized pores**. There are two types of polyps, **sensory/stinging (dactylozooids)** and **feeding (gastrozooids).** The feeding polyps are stout and encircled by five to nine tall, thin sensory/stinging polyps. The polyp's gastric cavities are interconnected beneath the skeletal surface. Fire corals are generally tan to mustard with white at the tips or edges of the skeletal structure.

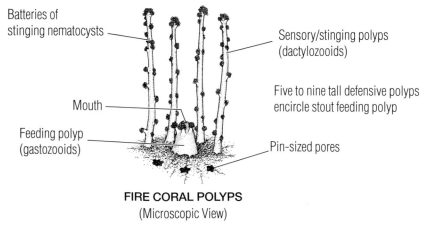

Batteries of stinging nematocysts

Sensory/stinging polyps (dactylozooids)

Five to nine tall defensive polyps encircle stout feeding polyp

Mouth

Feeding polyp (gastozooids)

Pin-sized pores

FIRE CORAL POLYPS
(Microscopic View)

There are four growth patterns in the Caribbean — **branching, blade, ridged** and **box;** all often encrust. Many scientists believe these represent four distinct species, others contend, however, that branching, blade and labyrinth are simply growth form of the same species and only box is a second distinct species.

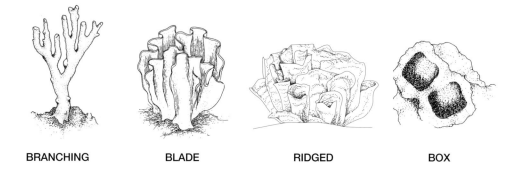

BRANCHING   BLADE   RIDGED   BOX

Lace Corals

ORDER: Anthoathecata (An-thuh-A-thee-cot-a/ L. flower and unsheathed)
SUBORDER: Filifera (Fill-ih-FUR-a / L. thread-bearing)
FAMILY: Stylasteridae (Sty-LASS-ter-ih-dee / Gr. a pillar, and a star)

The common name "lace coral" is derived from their profusely branched, hard calcareous skeleton. The polyps extend through pores in the calcareous skeleton and form small cup-like structures, similar in appearance to those of stony corals. These tiny cups give outer branches a **serrated appearance.** Occasional cups are also visible on the branches' thick bases. Lace corals are usually shades of purple, burgundy or lavender at the base, fading to pink and white toward the branches' tips. There is only one species in the Caribbean.

Unlike fire corals, lace corals lack the powerful batteries of stinging nematocysts. They are not generally considered toxic to divers, although contact can irritate sensitive skin.

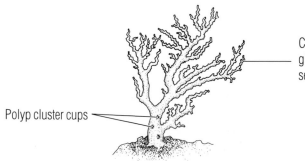

Clustered polyp cups give outer branches serrated appearance

Polyp cluster cups

LACE CORAL

VISUAL ID: Colonies form multiple branched structure. Branches generally cylindrical. Most commonly branch in a single plane, but occasionally in multiple directions. Often encrust and overgrow gorgonian colonies, taking on their shape. Surface texture smooth with numerous pin-hole pores. When the tiny polyps protrude, they appear as short, fine hairs. Tan to mustard and brown; branch tips white.

ABUNDANCE & DISTRIBUTION: Abundant to common Florida, Bahamas, Caribbean.

HABITAT & BEHAVIOR: Inhabit numerous marine habitats. The only one of the four fire corals that commonly grows deeper than 30 feet; relatively uncommon in shallow surge zones.

EFFECT ON DIVERS: Toxic; contact with bare skin will produce an intense, but usually short-lived, sting. May cause minor redness, welts and rash.

Branching Fire Coral
*Encrusting
sea feather plume.*

BRANCHING FIRE CORAL
Millepora alcicornis
SUBORDER:
Capitata
FAMILY:
Milleporidae

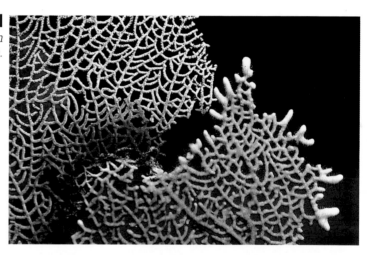

SIZE: 1 - 18 in.
DEPTH: 3 - 130 ft.

Branching Fire Coral
*Encrusting common
sea fan.*

Growth variations.
[below left page]
*Branches extending from
encrusted substrate.*
[below left]
Hair-like polyp detail.
[below right]

Fire Corals

VISUAL ID: Colonies form thin, upright blades or plates that extend from an encrusting base. Outer edge of blades uneven with multiple extensions or short branches. Surface texture smooth with numerous pin-hole pores. When the tiny polyps protrude, they appear as short, fine hair. Tan to mustard and brown; blade edges white.

ABUNDANCE & DISTRIBUTION: Abundant to common Florida, Bahamas, Caribbean.

HABITAT & BEHAVIOR: Inhabit shallow water reef tops. Usually in areas with some water movement; most common in areas with constant surge.

EFFECT ON DIVERS: Toxic; contact with bare skin will produce an intense, but usually short-lived sting. May cause minor redness, welts and rash.

Blade Fire Coral
Often mix on reef tops with several species of true stony corals.

**BLADE
FIRE CORAL**
Millepora complanata

SUBORDER:
Capitata
FAMILY:
Milleporidae

SIZE: 1 - 18 in.
DEPTH: 0 - 45 ft.

Blade Fire Coral
*Hair-like
polyp detail.*

Blade Fire Coral
*Often mix on shallow coral
heads with several species of
true stony corals and
gorgonians.*

Detail of growth variations.
[left page]

19

VISUAL ID: Form encrusting plates on the substrate. Thin upright blades with vertical ridges that become more distinct toward the upper ends of the blades. Blades of many colonies join to form labyrinth patterns that can be quite intricate; other colonies form lacy branching paddle-like or triangular blades. Surface texture smooth with numerous pin-hole pores. When the tiny polyps protrude, they appear as short, fine haris. Tan to mustard and brown; blade edges and occasionally ridge edges white.

ABUNDANCE & DISTRIBUTION: Uncommon to rare coastal Central and South America from Belize to Venezuela including offshore islands.

HABITAT & BEHAVIOR: Most common on shallow turbid inshore areas, also inhabit areas of seagrass and rubble.

EFFECT ON DIVERS: Toxic; contact with bare skin will produce an intense, but usually short-lived sting. May cause minor redness, welts and rash.

Ridged Fire Coral
Intricate labyrinth pattern.

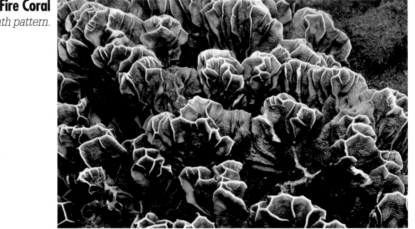

Ridged Fire Coral
Unusual fan-like blade tips.

**RIDGED
FIRE CORAL**
Millepora striata
SUBORDER:
Capitata
FAMILY:
Milleporidae

SIZE: 1 - 8 in.
DEPTH: 3 - 30 ft.

Ridged Fire Coral
*Colony with only sparse
upright blades.*

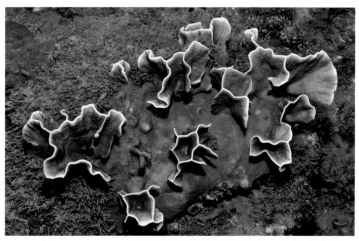

Small colony.
[below left]
Unusual labyrinth pattern.
[below right]

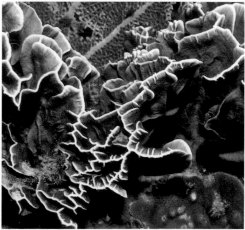

Variations of Fire Coral Growth Pattern

Occasionally Branching, Blade, and Ridged Fire Coral grow in atypical patterns that make visual identification to species difficult. At times different species display similar growth patterns. These similarities have caused some coral scientists to speculate that the three species of fire coral might actually be a single species with extremely plastic growth forms; others believe that the three species may occasionally hybridize producing different variations and similar visual characteristics. Examples of unusual growth patterns appear below.

Fire Coral Variation

Possible hybrid of Blade and Branching Fire Corals, or unusual variation of either species.

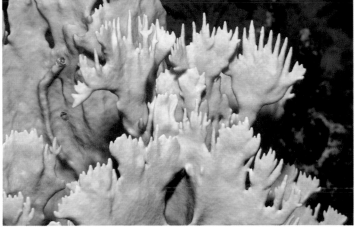

Fire Coral Variation

Possible hybrid of Blade and Ridged Fire Corals, or unusual variation of either species.

Possible hybrid of Blade and Branching Fire Corals, or unusual variation of either species. [left]

Fire Coral Variation

Possibly hybrid of Blade and Branching Fire Corals, or unusual variation of either species.

Possible hybrid of Blade and Branching Fire Corals, or unusual variation of either species. [left]

Fire Corals

VISUAL ID: Colonies form open-ended, thick-walled, box-like structures that extend upward from an encrusting base. Often join to form honeycomb pattern, or encrust in rippled wave-like pattern. Surface texture smooth with numerous pin-hole pores. When the tiny polyps protrude, they appear as short, fine hairs. Tan to mustard brown with reddish to pink or lavender tints that are distinctive of species; open end edges of boxes whitish.

ABUNDANCE & DISTRIBUTION: Occasional Dominican Republic to Puerto Rico, Lesser Antilles and Venezuela. Not reported Florida, Bahamas, North or West Caribbean.

HABITAT & BEHAVIOR: Inhabit shallow reef tops. Usually in areas with some water movement, especially surge zones.

EFFECT ON DIVERS: Not considered toxic; although may sting sensitive skin.

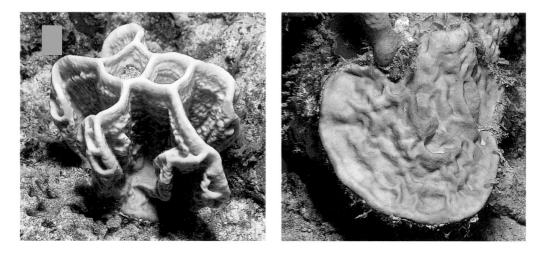

BOX FIRE CORAL
Millepora squarrosa
SUBORDER:
Capitata
FAMILY:
Milleporidae

SIZE: ¹/₂ - 2 in.
DEPTH: 6 - 30 ft.

Box Fire Coral
Growth variations.

VISUAL ID: Colonies form fan-like structures of branches. The cylindrical branches taper from base to tip. Tiny cups, formed by the feeding polyps and the encircling stinging polyps, give outer branches a serrated appearance. Occasional cups also visible on branches' thick base. Polyps have translucent hair-like appearance when extended. Small, hemispherical bumps occasionally grow on branches. Purple to burgundy or lavender near colony base fading to pink and white toward branch tips. Occasionally all white.

ABUNDANCE & DISTRIBUTION: Common South Florida, Bahamas, Caribbean.

HABITAT & BEHAVIOR: Inhabit protected, shaded areas of reefs. Often beneath ledge overhangs, inside cracks, caves and recesses.

EFFECT ON DIVERS: Not considered toxic, although may sting sensitive skin.

ROSE LACE CORAL
Stylaster roseus

SUBORDER:
Filifera
FAMILY:
Stylasteridae

SIZE: 1 - 4 in.
DEPTH: 15 - 100 ft.

Rose Lace Coral
Color variations.

Rose Lace Coral
Color variation.

Growing on sponge. [far left]
Growing on Branching Fire Coral. [left]

Class Anthozoa

(An-thuh-ZO-uh / L. flower-like animal)

Subclass Octocorallia

(Octo-core-AL-ee-uh / Gr. & L. eight and coral animal)

Gorgonians, Telestaceans, Soft Corals

Octocorallian polyps have **eight tentacles** that bear tiny pinnate (feather-like) projections called **pinnules.** Octocoral colors come from one or a combination of three sources: pigments in the polyps' tissues; intracellular symbiotic algae in the polyps' tissues, called zooxanthellae (zo-zan-THEL-ee); and/or coloring minerals in the calcareous spicules of the colonial structure. Colors often vary between colonies of the same species and are rarely useful in the identification process. For those few species where color is a reliable identification characteristic, a dive light is necessary to reveal the true shade underwater. Occasionally, members of this subclass are inaccurately referred to as horny corals because their supporting skeletal material superficially resembles the horn-like protein of turtle shells, and the hoofs, horns, and antlers of mammals.

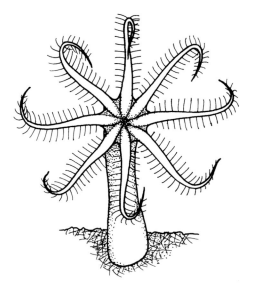

OCTOCORALLIAN POLYP

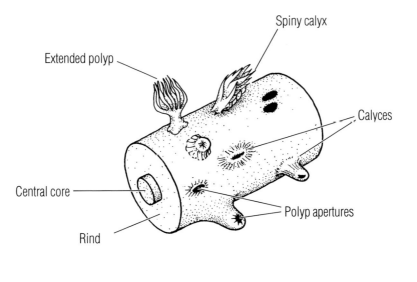

Spiny calyx

Extended polyp

Calyces

Central core

Polyp apertures

Rind

GORGONIAN BRANCH
(Showing calyx and aperture variations)

Gorgonians

Traditionally ORDER: Gorgonacea

(Gore-GON-ace-ee-ah / Gr. ugly, terrible or myth of three sisters with snakes for hair)

SUBORDERS: Scleraxonia and Holaxonia

Gorgonians is the preferred name for this large group of octocorallians; however, they are commonly called soft corals because of the colonies' lack of a hard, rigid, permanent skeletons. The common name soft coral should be used when referring to members of the Family Nephtheidae, abundant in the Indo-Pacific. Gorgonians include the animal colonies known as sea rods, flat sea whips, sea feather plumes, sea fans and orange sea whips. To assist in visual identification, species have been arranged by the colony's shape and common name, rather than their traditional scientific grouping. In most instances this method keeps members of the same family and genus together.

The stems and branches of all gorgonians have a central skeleton or axis. The **central core** in the Suborder Scleraxonia is composed of either tightly bound or fused calcareous spicules. A wood-like core typifies the Suborder Holaxonia. The core is surrounded by gelatinous material called the **rind. Polyps** are embedded in the rind and extend their tentacles and bodies from surface openings (apertures). The arrangement of the polyps (in rows, alternating bands, randomly scattered, etc.) is often helpful in the identification process. The shape of **polyp apertures** and the rims around them, called **calyces (calyx, singular),** are often used to determine the genus and, occasionally, species.

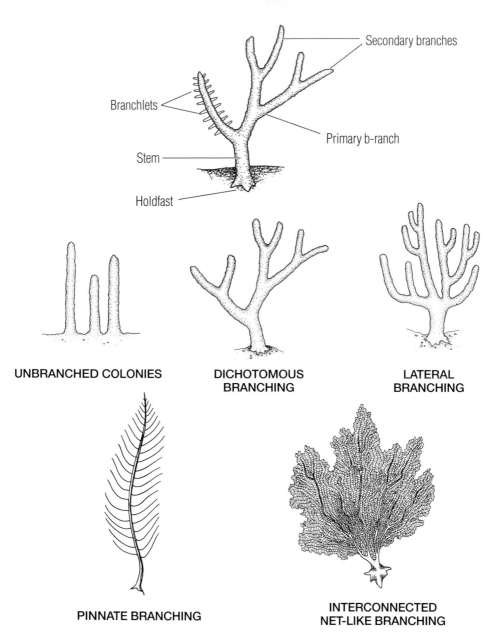

Secondary branches

Branchlets

Primary b-ranch

Stem

Holdfast

UNBRANCHED COLONIES

DICHOTOMOUS BRANCHING

LATERAL BRANCHING

PINNATE BRANCHING

INTERCONNECTED NET-LIKE BRANCHING

Most gorgonian colonies are attached to the substrate by a single **holdfast** at the base of a stem that usually **branches.** This branching pattern, which includes **unbranched, dichotomous, lateral** and **pinnate branching** and **interconnected net-like branching,** is often characteristic of the genus and is occasionally distinctive in determining a species. Branching may be in a single plane or bushy. **Branchlets** are small, usually profuse, branches that in some species line the sides of the **primary branches.**

Unfortunately, less than half of the 60-70 reef gorgonians can be visually identified to species underwater. Positive identification requires microscopic examination of the location, pattern, shape and size of the skeletal spicules embedded in the polyp's and colony's common tissue.

30

Telestaceans

ORDER: Alcyonacea – SUBORDER: Stolonifera
FAMILY: Clavulariidae – SUBFAMILY: Telestinae
Traditionally **ORDER Telestacea** (Tell-uh-STAY-see-ah / Gr. poet)

Telestacean colonies grow by extending a long **terminal polyp** that produces a stem with short side branches tipped with **daughter polyps.** The polyps are brilliant white. They can often be identified by stem color, depth and geographical location. The stem's color, however, is frequently obscured by encrusting algae, sponge, and other organisms. Telestaceans are generally found in areas of moderate turbidity, and only rarely occur on clear water reefs. They are considered a fouling organism.

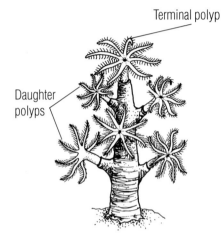

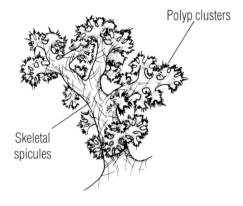

TELESTACEAN COLONY

SOFT CORAL COLONY

Soft Corals

ORDER: Alcyonacea (Al-see-uh-NAY-see-ah /Gr. a kingfisher)
FAMILY: Nephtheidae (NEF-the-ih-dee / Gr. lady of the house)

Soft corals resemble thick-trunked, branched trees. **Polyps** are clumped on the branch tips, and occasionally in small clusters and/or solitary polyps on the trunk or branches' surface. The pliable colony is composed of a rubbery or thick jelly-like material that is often translucent with the embedded **skeletal spicules** clearly visible. Colors are a wide range of pastel shades. Although profuse on Indo-Pacific reefs, there are only a few species in the Tropical Western Atlantic and these usually occur far below safe diving limits. On occasion, however, a few colonies may grow as shallow as 100 feet.

Gorgonians

VISUAL ID: Colonies form one to several erect, unbranched, cylindrical rods that extend from a common encrusting base. When extended large polyps give colony "hairy" appearance. Area around pore-like polyp apertures often swollen. Rods (rind) violet to purple and purple-gray, occasionally with some tints of brown or tan; polyps greenish brown to brown and brownish gray. Colonies also form thick encrustations without any erect rod structures. Occasionally encrust branches of other gorgonians. (Compare similar-appearing Encrusting Gorgonian, *Erythropodium caribaeoru*, distinguished by tan rind and polyps.)

ABUNDANCE & DISTRIBUTION: Abundant to common South Florida, Bahamas, Caribbean.

HABITAT & BEHAVIOR: Inhabit most reef environments, especially shallow fringing, patch and back reef areas.

NOTE: Also commonly known as Deadman's Fingers.

Corky Sea Finger
Comparison of colonies with polyps extended and retracted; note purplish shades of rind.

CORKY SEA FINGER
Briareum asbestinum

SUBORDER:
Scleraxonia
FAMILY:
Briareidae

SIZE: Colony height
¹/₂ - 24 in.
DEPTH: 3 - 100 ft.

Corky Sea Finger
*Colony encrusting
sea feather plume.*

Corky Sea Finger
*Comparison of colony with
polyps extended and
retracted.*

*Polyp detail;
Encrusting variation.*
[far left]

Encrusting large area.
[left]

Gorgonians

VISUAL ID: Colonies form encrusting mats. Extended polyps and tentacles appear as fine hairs. When polyps retracted rind appears smooth and leather-like, and apertures appear as pin-hole pores, rarely with slightly projecting calyces. Tan, underside reddish, apertures often whitish. (Similar encrusting variation of Corky Sea Finger, *Briarum asbestium*, [previous] distinguished by thick, purplish rind and larger, darker polyps, often area around polyp apertures swollen.)

ABUNDANCE & DISTRIBUTION: Occasional Florida, Bahamas, Caribbean.

HABITAT & BEHAVIOR: Encrust over hard substrate in most reef environments, especially shallow fringing, patch and back reef areas.

Encrusting Gorgonian
Note fine "hair-like" appearance of extended polyps.

VISUAL ID: Colonies are quite bushy, but grow in flat vertical planes. Tend to branch laterally with only occasional dichotomous branching. (Similar Bent Sea Rod, *Plexaura flexuosa,* [next] tends to branch dichotomously.) The contrast of light yellow-brown to brown polyps against dark brown to black stalks (rind) is a distinctive characteristic of this species. When polyps retracted area around apertures is flat or protrudes only slightly.

ABUNDANCE & DISTRIBUTION: Common South Florida, Bahamas, Caribbean.

HABITAT & BEHAVIOR: Inhabit clear water patch reefs. Colonies growing in deeper water tend to have more slender branches in denser concentrations and grow taller than their shallow water counterparts.

ENCRUSTING GORGONIAN
Erythropodium
caribaeorum
SUBORDER:
Scleraxonia
FAMILY:
Anthothelidae

SIZE: 3 in. - 3 ft.
DEPTH: 3 - 100 ft.

Encrusting Gorgonian
Comparison of extended
and retracted polyps; note
smooth texture of rind.

BLACK SEA ROD
Plexaura homomalla
SUBORDER:
Holaxonia
FAMILY:
Plexauridae

SIZE: Colony height
$^1/_2$ - 2 ft.
DEPTH: 4 - 200 ft.

continued next page

Gorgonians

Black Sea Rod

Branch detail with polyps retracted.

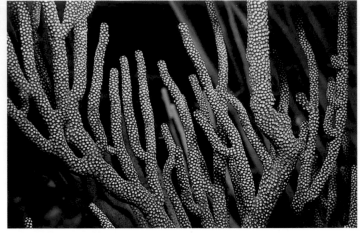

VISUAL ID: Colonies usually grow in flat vertical planes with profuse dichotomous branching. (Similar Black Sea Rod, *Plexaura homomalla,* [previous] tends to branch laterally.) Occasionally bushy, branching in all directions. Pale to tan, yellow-brown, brown, reddish purple and purple. Polyps occasionally lighter shade than stalk. When polyps retracted rim of aperture is only slightly raised with a small lip or shelf around the inside.

ABUNDANCE & DISTRIBUTION: Common South Florida, Bahamas, Caribbean.

HABITAT & BEHAVIOR: Inhabit clear water patch reefs.

NOTE: Previously classified in the genus *Plexaura.*

Bent Sea Rod

Branch detail with polyps retracted.

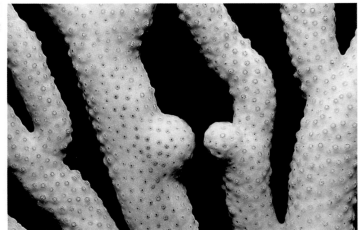

Black Sea Rod
continued from previous page

Small colony branch detail with polyps extended.

BENT SEA ROD
Eunicea flexuosa

SUBORDER:
Holaxonia
FAMILY:
Plexauridae

SIZE: Colony height
6 - 16 in.
DEPTH: 4 - 150 ft.

Bent Sea Rod
Branching in multiple directions.

Gorgonians

VISUAL ID: Sea rod colonies of this genus can be recognized when their polyps are retracted by noting apertures that appear as round to oval pores without raised rims (calyces). All four species in this genus are so similar in appearance that they cannot easily be visually identified to species. Microscopic examination is required for positive identification. Colonies are generally bushy with stout stalks and branch dichotomously. Colors vary greatly from light brown to yellow-brown, brown, reddish purple, purple and gray.

ABUNDANCE & DISTRIBUTION: Common South Florida, Bahamas, Caribbean.

HABITAT & BEHAVIOR: Inhabit most clear water reefs.

Porous Sea Rods
Note pore-like polyp apertures without raised calyces.

POROUS SEA RODS
Pseudoplexaura spp.

SUBORDER:
Holaxonia
FAMILY:
Plexauridae

SIZE: Colony height
$^1/_2$ - 7 ft.
DEPTH: 3 - 250 ft.

Porous Sea Rods
Note pore-like polyp apertures.

Tall colony.
[far left]

Branch detail.
[left]

Porous Sea Rods
Bush-like colony.

Gorgonians

VISUAL ID: Sea rod colonies of this genus can be recognized when their polyps are retracted leaving prominently extended calyces (with the exception of *E. knighti* that has polyp apertures resembling those of Porous Sea Rods). Most branch laterally in a flat plane resembling candelabra. Only a few of the more than a dozen genus members can be distinguished to species underwater. The remaining species are so similar in appearance that microscopic examinations are required for positive identification. Colors vary greatly from light brown through yellow-brown, brown, reddish purple, purple and gray.

ABUNDANCE & DISTRIBUTION: Common South Florida, Bahamas, Caribbean.

HABITAT & BEHAVIOR: Inhabit most reef habitats and adjacent sandy substrates.

Knobby Sea Rods
Polyp detail.

VISUAL ID: The close-set, swollen, tubular calyces of these candelabrum-shaped colonies easily distinguish them from other members of the genus. Colonies compact with stout branches. Light yellowish brown.

ABUNDANCE & DISTRIBUTION: Common Northwest Caribbean; uncommon to occasional South Florida, Bahamas, eastern and southern Caribbean.

HABITAT & BEHAVIOR: Inhabit most reef environments from shallow, turbulent hard bottoms to patch reefs, deeper outer reefs and along wall lips.

SIMILAR SPECIES: Tube-knob Candelabrum, *Eunicea laxispica,* distinguished by longer, more widely spaced, tube-like calyces. Uncommon to rare.

KNOBBY SEA RODS
Eunicea spp.
SUBORDER:
Holaxonia
FAMILY:
Plexauridae

SIZE: Colony height
$^1/_2$ - 3 ft.
DEPTH: 3 - 100 ft.

Knobby Sea Rods
Knobby calyx detail.

SWOLLEN-KNOB CANDELABRUM
Eunicea mammosa
SUBORDER:
Holaxonia
FAMILY:
Plexauridae

SIZE: Colony height
$^3/_4$ - 1 ft.
DEPTH: 5 - 90 ft.

continued next page 41

Swollen-knob Candelabrum

Calyx detail; note close-set, swollen tubular form.

VISUAL ID: The diagonally upward projecting calyces distinguish this species from other members of the genus. In side view the calyces appear as tiny shelves with diagonal supports. Calyces' lower lips slightly upturned. Colonies grow in two forms: form *succinea* are low, wide, candelabrum-shaped with thick end branches; form *plantaginea* are tall and bushy with thin end branches, calyces' lower lips more upturned. (Similar Warty Sea Rod, *Eunicea calyculata*, [next] distinguished by thicker branches and gaping calyces.) Light yellowish brown to brown.

ABUNDANCE & DISTRIBUTION: Common South Florida, Bahamas, Caribbean.

HABITAT & BEHAVIOR: Inhabit shallow, turbulent hard bottoms and patch reefs.

Shelf-knob Sea Rod

Calyx detail; note shelf-like appearance.

Swollen-knob Candelabrum

continued from previous page

Colony with polyps retracted.

SHELF-KNOB SEA ROD
Eunicea succinea

SUBORDER:
Holaxonia
FAMILY:
Plexauridae

Form *succinea.*

SIZE: Colony height
³/₄ - 2 ft.
DEPTH: 5 - 50 ft.

Shelf-knob Sea Rod
Form *plantaginea.*

VISUAL ID: Only species in genus *Eunicea* with thick cylindrical, non-tapering branches that is tall, bushy, and does not branch in a single plane. (Similar to Shelf-knob Sea Rod, *Eunicea succinea*, form *plantaginea* [previous], that is distinguished by thinner end branches and shelf-like calyces.) Dichotomous branching. Extended polyps give colony yellowish brown appearance. Calyces low and gaping.

ABUNDANCE & DISTRIBUTION: Common South Florida, Bahamas, Caribbean.

HABITAT & BEHAVIOR: Inhabit many reef environments; most common on inshore reefs.

Warty Sea Rod
Polyp detail.

VISUAL ID: When fully contracted the low, circular, somewhat swollen calyces with round central apertures distinguish this species from other members of the genus. Often form low, bushy, shrub-like colonies, occasionally tall with widely spaced branches. Rods light to dark gray; polyps yellow-brown to brown.

ABUNDANCE & DISTRIBUTION: Common to occasional South Florida, Bahamas, Caribbean.

HABITAT & BEHAVIOR: Inhabit shallow, turbulent hard bottoms and patch reefs.

WARTY SEA ROD
Eunicea calyculata
SUBORDER:
Holaxonia
FAMILY:
Plexauridae

SIZE: Colony height
1 - 3 ft.
DEPTH: 10 - 110 ft.

Warty Sea Rod
Calyx detail.

DOUGHNUT SEA ROD
Eunicea fusca
SUBORDER:
Holaxonia
FAMILY:
Plexauridae

SIZE: Colony height
$1/2$ - $1 1/2$ ft.
DEPTH: 10 - 75 ft.

continued next page **45**

Gorgonians

VISUAL ID: Sea rod colonies of this genus can be recognized when their polyps are retracted, leaving elliptical or slit-like apertures that may or may not have slightly raised rims (calyces). With one exception, Giant Slit-pore Sea Rod, *Plexaurella nutans,* [next], all the species in genus *Plexaurella* are so similar in appearance that microscopic examinations are required for positive identification. Colonies are generally bushy with stout stalks, and branch dichotomously. Colors vary greatly from light brown to yellow-brown, brown, reddish purple, purple and gray.

ABUNDANCE & DISTRIBUTION: Common South Florida, Bahamas, Caribbean.

HABITAT & BEHAVIOR: Inhabit most clear water reef environments.

Slit-pore Sea Rods
Colony with polyps retracted.

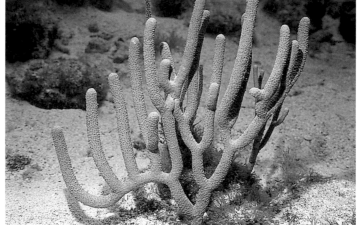

Doughnut Sea Rod
*continued from
previous page*

*Comparison of
Doughnut Sea Rod, (left)
and Bent Sea Rod (right).*

Polyp detail.
[far left]

Calyx detail.
[left]

**SLIT-PORE
SEA RODS**
Plexaurella spp.
SUBORDER:
Holaxonia
FAMILY:
Plexauridae

SIZE: Colony height
$^1/_2$ - 3$^1/_2$ ft.
DEPTH: 3 - 160 ft.

Slit-pore Sea Rods
*Retracted polyp detail;
note slit-like aperture.*

VISUAL ID: Colonies tall with thick stalks and sparse dichotomous branching. Branch tips usually somewhat enlarged. Slit-like apertures of retracted polyps are slightly raised, well-separated mounds. Pale gray to tan or light brown.

ABUNDANCE & DISTRIBUTION: Common to occasional South Florida, Bahamas, Caribbean.

HABITAT & BEHAVIOR: Primarily inhabit clear water patch and fore reefs.

NOTE: Also commonly known as Nodding Plexaurella.

Giant Slit-pore Sea Rod

Retracted polyp detail; note slightly raised lips and slit-like pores.

VISUAL ID: Low, broad fan-shaped colonies branch laterally with only occasional dichotomous secondary branching in single planes. Branches tend to be compact. Hard, rough calyces with sharply spiked tips extend prominently. Pale yellowish brown to light brown; polyps white.

ABUNDANCE & DISTRIBUTION: Common to occasional South Florida, Bahamas, Caribbean.

HABITAT & BEHAVIOR: Wide range of shallow to moderate habitats.

NOTE: Photographed specimen was collected and visual identification confirmed by examination of wood-like central branch axis which is conspicuously flattened in this species.

SIMILAR SPECIES: Open Spiny Sea Fan, *M. atlantica,* visually distinguished by their tendency to be taller and having more open branching. Uncommon. Positive identification requires specimen examination of the wood-like central branch axis which is not conspicuously flattened.

**GIANT SLIT-PORE
SEA ROD**
Plexaurella nutans
SUBORDER:
Holaxonia
FAMILY:
Plexauridae

SIZE: Colony height
2 - 4½ ft.
DEPTH: 30 - 160 ft.

SPINY SEA FAN
Muricea muricata
SUBORDER:
Holaxonia
FAMILY:
Plexauridae

SIZE: Colony height
4 - 12 in.
DEPTH: 0 - 60 ft.

continued next page

Gorgonians

VISUAL ID: Colonies have open pinnate branching in single planes; older colonies may be somewhat bushy. Branchlets short, stiff and widely spaced. Hard, rough calyces; each has a distinctive, long, sharp terminal spine. Branches whitish to light gray or yellow-brown; polyps yellowish brown. (Similar Pinnate Spiny Sea Fan, *Muricea pendula*, is described on page 83 because of its distinctive red color.)

ABUNDANCE & DISTRIBUTION: Occasional Caribbean.

HABITAT & BEHAVIOR: Inhabit clear water, moderate to deep fore reefs.

Long Spine Sea Fan
Branch/polyp detail; note open pinnate branching.

Spiny Sea Fan
*continued from
previous page*

Unusually tall colony.

*Polyp detail.
[far left]*

*Calyx detail.
[left]*

LONG SPINE SEA FAN
Muricea pinnata
SUBORDER:
Holaxonia
FAMILY:
Plexauridae

SIZE: Colony height
8 - 18 in.
DEPTH: 40 - 120 ft.

Long Spine Sea Fan
*Branch/calyx detail;
note long, terminal spines.*

Gorgonians

VISUAL ID: Tall, bushy colonies, not branched in single planes. Branch laterally near base, but toward top tend to branch pinnately. Hard, rough, close-set calyces with sharply spiked lower lips extend prominently. Branches yellow to yellowish brown, orange or amber; polyps white. (Similar Delicate Spiny Sea Rod, *Muricea laxa*, [next] can usually be distinguished by thinner bluish white to gray branches, more projecting calyx lips, and deeper habitat.)

ABUNDANCE & DISTRIBUTION: Common to occasional Florida's west coast and from West Palm on Florida's east coast south through the Keys, Bahamas, Caribbean.

HABITAT & BEHAVIOR: Inhabit wide range of shallow to moderate environments from sandy bottoms to sloping rocky substrates and patch reefs.

NOTE: Small sample of pictured specimen was collected and visual identification confirmed by microscopic examination of spicules.

Orange Spiny Sea Rod
Polyp detail.

VISUAL ID: Tall, bushy colonies, laterally branched, but not in single planes. Branches slender, flexible and long. Narrow, hard, rough calyces extend prominently upward with sharply spiked lower lips. Branches bluish gray to bluish white, occasionally yellowish; polyps white. (Compare similar Orange Spiny Sea Rod, *M. elongata*, [previous].)

ABUNDANCE & DISTRIBUTION: Common to occasional Florida's west coast and from West Palm on Florida's east coast south through the Keys, Bahamas.

HABITAT & BEHAVIOR: Inhabit wide range of moderate to deep environments from sloping rocky substrates to patch reefs.

NOTE: Small sample of pictured specimen was collected and visual identification confirmed by microscopic examination of spicules.

ORANGE SPINY SEA ROD
Muricea elongata
SUBORDER:
Holaxonia
FAMILY:
Plexauridae

SIZE: Colony height
1 - 1 ½ ft.
DEPTH: 10 - 70 ft.

Orange Spiny Sea Rod
Branch/calyx detail; note orangish color.

DELICATE SPINY SEA ROD
Muricea laxa
SUBORDER:
Holaxonia
FAMILY:
Plexauridae

SIZE: Colony height
8 - 12 in.
DEPTH: 60 - 420 ft.

continued next page **53**

Gorgonians

VISUAL ID: Colonies form bushy clusters of tall, plume-like branches. Numerous short, slender, round branchlets extend from all sides of main branches. Small, closely set polyp apertures are scattered randomly on all sides of main and secondary branches. (Similar Sea Plumes, *Antillogorgia* spp., [next] have polyps in rows, series or bands.) Apertures have small, lower shelf-like lips, giving the surface a somewhat rough texture. Most commonly purple, occasionally gray, and may be tinged with yellow.

ABUNDANCE & DISTRIBUTION: Common South Florida, Bahamas, Caribbean.

HABITAT & BEHAVIOR: Inhabit most clear water patch reef environments.

SIMILAR SPECIES: Sulphur Sea Plume, *Muricea sulphurea,* yellow, low, bushy, shrub-like colonies; secondary branches on all sides of main branches and polyps randomly scattered on all sides; Puerto Rico through Lesser Antilles. Deep Water Sea Plume, *M. petila,* tall, main branches with widely spaced, pinnately branching secondary branches; violet to lavender; below 100 feet; South Florida, Bahamas.

Rough Sea Plume

*Branch detail;
note branchlets
extending in
multiple directions.*

**Delicate Spiny
Sea Rod**

*continued from
previous page*

*Branch/calyx detail;
note bluish gray color.*

ROUGH SEA PLUME
Muriceopsis flavida
SUBORDER:
Holaxonia
FAMILY:
Plexauridae

SIZE: Colony height
8 - 30 in.
DEPTH: 3 - 110 ft.

Rough Sea Plume
Gray variation.

Gorgonians

VISUAL ID: Bushy clusters of tall, feather-like plumes typify this genus. Pinnate secondary branches extend from primary branches. Polyps in rows, series or bands rather of being randomly distributed on all sides of branches. Calyces absent or indistinct. Most commonly purple to gray branches, occasionally bright to pale yellow or yellow-brown. Polyps generally cream to brownish or grayish. With two exceptions, Slimy Sea Plume, *Antillogorgia americana,* [next] and Bipinnate Sea Plume, *A. bipinnata,* [next page], all of the remaining dozen or so species in this genus are so similar in appearance that they cannot easily be distinguished visually. Microscopic examination is required for positive identification.

ABUNDANCE & DISTRIBUTION: Common South Florida, Bahamas, Caribbean.

HABITAT & BEHAVIOR: Inhabit most reef environments from shallow, seaward sandy areas to patch reefs and deep clear water reefs along drop-offs.

Sea Plumes
Several species can exceed seven feet in height.

VISUAL ID: Colonies form bushy clusters of tall, feather-like plumes. Long branchlets extend pinnately from primary branches. Primary branches most commonly purple to violet, occasionally pale yellow. Living colonies produce large amounts of mucus causing the branches to feel slimy to the touch, a characteristic that helps distinguish this species other genus members. (To avoid injury to a colony it should only be lightly touched near the base, which will feel soft, slick and slimy.)

ABUNDANCE & DISTRIBUTION: Common South Florida, Bahamas, Caribbean.

HABITAT & BEHAVIOR: Inhabit most reef environments from shallow hard bottoms to patch and deep clear water reefs along drop-offs.

SEA PLUMES
Antillogorgia spp.
SUBORDER:
Holaxonia
FAMILY:
Gorgoniidae

SIZE: Colony height
1 - 7 ft.
DEPTH: 3 - 180 ft.

Sea Plumes
*Large colony
with polyps
retracted.*

SLIMY SEA PLUME
Antillogorgia americana
SUBORDER:
Holaxonia
FAMILY:
Gorgoniidae

SIZE: Colony height
2$^{1}/_{2}$ - 3$^{1}/_{2}$ ft.
DEPTH: 5 - 150 ft.

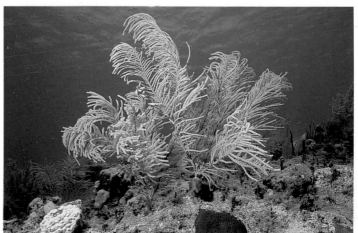

VISUAL ID: Colonies generally grow in single planes with broadly spread primary and secondary branches. Paired branchlets extend from branches at regularly intervals. These branchlets, distinctive of this species, are short, blunt, stiff and extend directly opposite one another at almost right angles. Branches most commonly purple to violet, occasionally bright yellow to whitish.

ABUNDANCE & DISTRIBUTION: Common South Florida, Bahamas, Caribbean.

HABITAT & BEHAVIOR: Inhabit moderate to deep clear water patch reefs.

VISUAL ID: Small, bushy and highly branched colonies. Branches quite flat and narrow with polyps extending from swollen, slit-like apertures along the thin edges. (Similar Grooved-blade Sea Whip, *Pterogorgia guadalupensis,* [next] is distinguished by polyps extending from a common groove along thin edges.) Branches bright yellow to green to olive with purple edges, occasionally all purple; polyps white to cream.

ABUNDANCE & DISTRIBUTION: Common South Florida, Bahamas, Caribbean. Can be abundant in localized areas.

HABITAT & BEHAVIOR: Inhabit a wide range of shallow inshore environments from back reefs to patch reefs.

BIPINNATE SEA PLUME
Antillogorgia bipinnata
SUBORDER:
Holaxonia
FAMILY:
Gorgoniidae

SIZE: Colony height
1 - 2 ft.
DEPTH: 45 - 180 ft.

Bipinnate Sea Plume
Colony with polyps retracted.

Branch detail with polyps extended.
[far left]

Branch detail with polyps retracted.
[left]

YELLOW SEA WHIP
Pterogorgia citrina
SUBORDER:
Holaxonia
FAMILY:
Gorgoniidae

SIZE: Colony height
4 - 12 in.
Branch width $1/4$ in.
DEPTH: 3 - 40 ft.

continued next page

Gorgonians

VISUAL ID: Colonies heavily branched in a more or less single planes. Long, flexible branches quite flat and wide, tapering somewhat from base to end. Polyps extend from a groove that runs along the thin edges. (Similar Yellow Sea Whip [previous] is distinguished by polyps extending from slit-like apertures along thin edges.) Branches olive to gray, occasionally light purple; polyps white to cream.

ABUNDANCE & DISTRIBUTION: Occasional South Florida, Bahamas, Caribbean.

HABITAT & BEHAVIOR: Inhabit a wide range of inshore environments from back reef areas of sand and rubble to patch reefs at moderate depth.

**Grooved-blade
Sea Whip**
Polyp/groove detail.

Yellow Sea Whip

continued from previous page

Color variation.

Calyx/polyp detail; note polyps do not extend from a slit-like groove. [far left]

Color variation. [left]

GROOVED-BLADE SEA WHIP

Pterogorgia guadalupensis

SUBORDER: Holaxonia
FAMILY: Gorgoniidae

SIZE: Colony height ½ - 2 ft.
Branch width ¼ - ½ in.
DEPTH: 3 - 60 ft.

Grooved-blade Sea Whip

Purplish variation.

VISUAL ID: Colonies large, bushy and highly branched. A cross-section of a branch is "Y" or "X" shaped. Branches taper from bases toward the terminal ends and are often twisted. Ends may occasionally be a flattened blade-shape. Polyps extend from a groove that runs along the branches' thin edges. Olive to brown to gray, occasionally purple or with purplish tints. Edge of grooves usually purple; polyps white to cream.

ABUNDANCE & DISTRIBUTION: Common to occasional South Florida, Bahamas, Caribbean. Can be abundant in localized areas.

HABITAT & BEHAVIOR: Inhabit a wide range of inshore environments from back reef areas of sand and rubble to patch reefs at moderate depth.

Angular Sea Whip
Polyp/groove detail.

VISUAL ID: Colonies form large fans that grow in single planes. Fans are composed of tightly-meshed, interconnected network of branches that are round or slightly flattened on the outer surface. (Compare similar Venus Sea Fan, *Gorgonia flabellum,* [next] that has inner edges distinctly flattened at right angles to fans' surfaces.) In Florida always purple, remainder of range commonly purple, but occasionally yellow or brownish.

ABUNDANCE & DISTRIBUTION: Common South Florida, Bahamas, Caribbean.

HABITAT & BEHAVIOR: Prefer clear water with some movement. Inhabit the seaward side of shallow reefs, slopes and patch reefs. Only occasionally on reefs and along the lips of drop-offs deeper than 50 feet.

ANGULAR SEA WHIP
Pterogorgia anceps
SUBORDER:
Holaxonia
FAMILY:
Gorgoniidae

SIZE: Colony height
1 - 2 ft.
Branch width ⅛ - ¼ in.
DEPTH: 12 - 65 ft.

Angular Sea Whip
*Colony with polyps
retracted.*

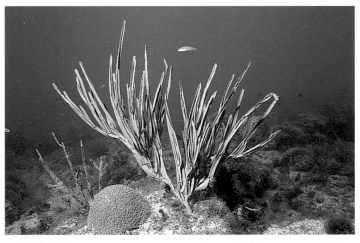

COMMON SEA FAN
Gorgonia ventalina
SUBORDER:
Holaxonia
FAMILY:
Gorgoniidae

SIZE: Colony height
2 - 6 ft.
DEPTH: 3 - 100 ft.

continued next page

Gorgonians

Common Sea Fan
*Branch detail;
outer surface flattened.*

VISUAL ID: Colonies form large fans that grow in single planes. Fans are composed of tightly-meshed, interconnected network of branches. Branches' inner edges are distinctly flattened at right angles to the fans' surfaces. (Compare similar Common Sea Fan, *Gorgonia ventalina,* [previous] that are rounded or slightly flattened on the outer surface.) Occasionally have small branchlets growing from their flat sides. Commonly yellow, occasionally lavender to gray.

ABUNDANCE & DISTRIBUTION: Abundant Bahamas; common to uncommon Caribbean; rare South Florida.

HABITAT & BEHAVIOR: Prefer clear water with some movement. Commonly inhabit the seaward side of shallow reef slopes and patch reefs. Only occasionally on reefs and along lips of drop-offs deeper than 35 feet. In Caribbean often inhabit shallow back reef areas.

NOTE: Also commonly known as Bahamian Sea Fan.

Venus Sea Fan
*Branch detail;
note branches inner edges
flattened at right angle
to fan's surface.*

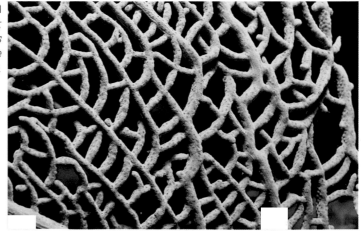

Common Sea Fan
continued from previous page

VENUS SEA FAN
Gorgonia flabellum
SUBORDER:
Holaxonia
FAMILY:
Gorgoniidae

SIZE: Colony height
2 - 3 ½ ft.
DEPTH: 3 - 100 ft.

Venus Sea Fan
Purple variation.

Gorgonians

VISUAL ID: Colonies form small fans that grow in single planes. Fans are composed of a widely meshed pattern of branches. Secondary branches extending from ascending primary branches are generally pinnate and do not always unite or interconnect. In deep water white to pale violet or yellow; in shallow water tend to be yellow occasionally with purplish tints.

ABUNDANCE & DISTRIBUTION: Occasional Caribbean. Not known from Florida or Bahamas.

HABITAT & BEHAVIOR: Prefer clear water with some movement. Inhabit wide range of reef environments, but most abundant below 50 feet where Common and Venus Sea Fans, *Gorgonia ventalina* and *G. flabellum*, [previous] are not as numerous.

Wide-mesh Sea Fan
*Branch structure detail;
note widely spaced
interconnecting branches.*

VISUAL ID: Huge fan-shaped colonies branch dichotomously in single planes. Outer surfaces of branches flattened with polyps extending in two parallel rows from narrow inner edges. Red-brown to orange-brown, dark brown and gray.

ABUNDANCE & DISTRIBUTION: Abundant to occasional East Florida, Bahamas, Caribbean.

HABITAT & BEHAVIOR: Inhabit most deep water environments from patch reefs to deep slopes, canyons, crevices and walls. Prefer clear water with some current. Most common below 60 feet. Polyps generally extended, especially when there is water movement.

WIDE-MESH SEA FAN
Gorgonia mariae
SUBORDER:
Holaxonia
FAMILY:
Gorgoniidae

SIZE: Colony height
6 - 12 in.
DEPTH: 3 - 156 ft.

Wide-mesh Sea Fan
Yellow variation.

DEEPWATER SEA FAN
Iciligorgia schrammi
SUBORDER:
Scleraxonia
FAMILY:
Anthothelidae

SIZE: Colony height
1 - 4 ft.
DEPTH: 35 - 1200 ft.

continued next page **67**

Gorgonians

Deepwater Sea Fan
Polyp detail.

VISUAL ID: Form both slender branching and stout rod-like colonies. Cone-shaped calyces protrude noticeably. Either red stems with red calyces; or red stems with yellow calyx rims; or yellow to orange stems with reddish, violet or purple calyx rims. Polyps white and somewhat translucent. (Stout rod-like colonies similar to Brilliant Sea Fingers, *Titanideum frauenfeldii,* [next] distinguished by smooth rod surfaces.)

ABUNDANCE & DISTRIBUTION: Common to occasional South Florida, Bahamas, Caribbean.

HABITAT & BEHAVIOR: Inhabit wide range of moderate to deep environments from patch reefs to sandy and rocky substrates to shaded areas under ledge overhangs along deep walls.

NOTE: A small sample of photographed specimen was collected and visual identification confirmed by microscopic examination of spicules.

Colorful Sea Rod
Branch/polyp detail.

Deepwater Sea Fan
continued from previous page

Colony with polyps extended.

COLORFUL SEA ROD
Diodogorgia nodulifera
SUBORDER:
Scleraxonia
FAMILY:
Anthothelidae

SIZE: Colony height
4 - 12 in.
DEPTH: 45 - 600 ft.

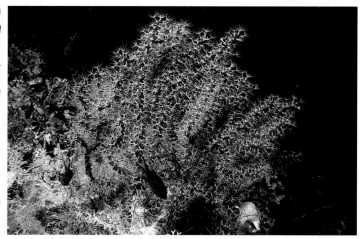

Colorful Sea Rod
Orange stem, reddish calyx variation.

VISUAL ID: Colonies usually form short, stout, smooth cylindrical rods; occasionally tall with several branches. Bright red to pinkish red, orange and yellowish orange; polyps translucent white.

ABUNDANCE & DISTRIBUTION: Occasional East Florida. Not reported Bahamas or Caribbean.

HABITAT & BEHAVIOR: Inhabit current-swept areas with hard, rocky substrates. Tend to be red off North Florida and orange off South Florida.

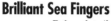

Brilliant Sea Fingers
Polyp detail.

VISUAL ID: Scraggly bushy, occasionally fan-shaped colonies with relatively thin branches and long protruding calyces. Only gorgonian in South Florida, Bahamas and Caribbean (within safe diving limits) with both orange to red stems and polyps.

ABUNDANCE & DISTRIBUTION: Common Florida; occasional to uncommon Bahamas, Caribbean.

HABITAT & BEHAVIOR: In Florida inhabit moderate to deep patch reefs and rocky/sandy substrates; colonies often quite bushy [opposite]. In Caribbean, tend to inhabit only deep water below 100 feet, especially under ledge overhangs and cave ceilings; colonies often in fan-like growth pattern [next page, right].

BRILLIANT SEA FINGERS
Titanideum frauenfeldii

SUBORDER:
Scleraxonia
FAMILY:
Anthothelidae

SIZE: Colony height
3 in. - 2 ft.
DEPTH: 50 - 780 ft.

Brilliant Sea Fingers
Typical rod-like colonies.

RED POLYP OCTOCORAL
Swiftia exserta

SUBORDER:
Holaxonia
FAMILY:
Plexauridae

SIZE: Colony height
6 - 18 in.
DEPTH: 40 - 260 ft.

continued next page **71**

Gorgonians

Red Polyp Octocoral
Polyp detail.

VISUAL ID: Colonies form single long, whip-like stalks that taper slightly from base to tip. Bright orange to orange-red to red; polyps white.

ABUNDANCE & DISTRIBUTION: Common to occasional East Florida, Bahamas, Caribbean.

HABITAT & BEHAVIOR: Inhabit deep, clear water environments, especially steep slopes and walls. Attach to rocky substrates.

Devil's Sea Whip
Polyp detail.

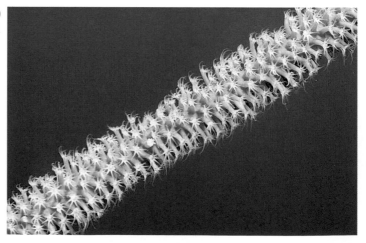

Red Polyp Octocoral
continued from previous page

Fan-like growth pattern.

DEVIL'S SEA WHIP
Ellisella barbadensis
SUBORDER:
Calcaxonia
FAMILY:
Ellisellidae

SIZE: Colony height
2 - 8 ft.
Base diameter
$1/4$ - $1/2$ in.
DEPTH: 65 - 1600 ft.

Gorgonians

VISUAL ID: Tall erect colonies branch dichotomously from short base stalks. Branches long, stiff, and whip-like. (Similar Bushy Sea Whip, *Ellisela schmitti*, [next page] occasionally grow upright, but are easily distinguished by their short branches that tend to rebranch several times.) Branches number from a few to over two dozen. Bright orange to orange-red to red; polyps white.

ABUNDANCE & DISTRIBUTION: Occasional Florida, Bahamas, Caribbean.

HABITAT & BEHAVIOR: Attach to rocky substrates in deep clear water environments, especially steep slopes and walls. In Caribbean most common below 100 feet, but as shallow as 50 feet along Florida's Gulf Coast.

SIMILAR SPECIES: At this time *E. grandis* is visually indistinguishable. Genus *Ellisella* needs further revision before identification is possible underwater.

Long Sea Whip
Polyp detail.

VISUAL ID: Fan-shaped colonies formed by some lateral branching off main stalks and profuse dichotomous rebranching in single planes. Bright orange to orange to red; polyps white.

ABUNDANCE & DISTRIBUTION: Occasional South Florida, Bahamas, Caribbean.

HABITAT & BEHAVIOR: Inhabit deep clear water environments, especially under ledge overhangs, on cave ceilings, inside crevices and along canyons and walls. Rare within safe diving limits.

74

LONG SEA WHIP
Ellisella elongata
SUBORDER:
Calcaxonia
FAMILY:
Ellisellidae

SIZE: Colony height
3 - 5 ft.
Base diameter
$^1/_4$ - $^1/_2$ in.
DEPTH: 50 - 720 ft.

**ORANGE DEEP
WATER FAN**
Nicella goreaui
SUBORDER:
Calcaxonia
FAMILY:
Ellisellidae

SIZE: Colony height
$^1/_2$ - 1$^1/_2$ ft.
DEPTH: 100 - 260 ft.

continued next page

Gorgonians

**Orange Deep
Water Fan**
Polyp detail.

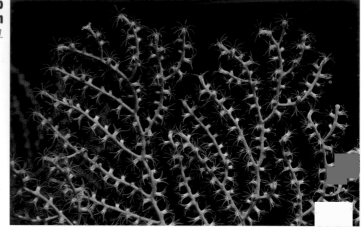

VISUAL ID: Numerous short stiff, whip-like branches and secondary branches extend from base stalks. (Similar Long Sea Whip, *Ellisella elongata,* [previous page] distinguished by branches that are long and generally without secondary branches.) Branching and rebranching are both lateral and dichotomous. Bright orange to orange to red; polyps white.

ABUNDANCE & DISTRIBUTION: Common to occasional South Florida, Bahamas, Caribbean.

HABITAT & BEHAVIOR: Inhabit deep clear water environments, especially under ledge overhangs, on cave ceilings, inside crevices and along canyons and walls. Rare within safe diving limits. Seldom grow upright like similar Long Sea Whip.

Orange Deep Water Fan
continued from previous page

Polyps retracted.

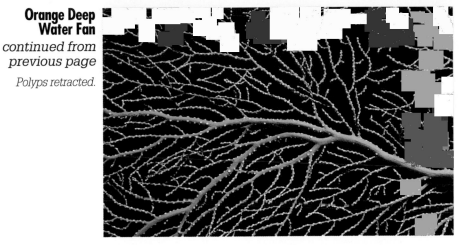

BUSHY SEA WHIP
Ellisella schmitti
SUBORDER:
Calcaxonia
FAMILY:
Ellisellidae

Polyp detail.
[far left]
Bushy branch detail.
[left]

SIZE: Colony height
1 - 2 ft.
Base diameter
$1/4$ - $1/2$ in.
DEPTH: 65 - 220 ft.

Gorgonians

VISUAL ID: Colonies form long straight, stiff, moderately branched whip-like stalks. Polyps in multiple rows along two sides. Calyces do not protrude when polyps are retracted. Stalks' color highly variable, including shades of lavender, violet, purple, red, orange, and yellow; polyps white.

ABUNDANCE & DISTRIBUTION: Common both coasts of Florida.

HABITAT & BEHAVIOR: Inhabit most environments, especially areas with hard substrate and some sand.

NOTE: Small sample of pictured specimen was collected and visual identification confirmed by microscopic examination of spicules. Formerly classified in genus *Lophogorgia*, which is no longer considered valid.

Colorful Sea Whip
Orange variation.

Colorful Sea Whip
Branch/polyp detail.

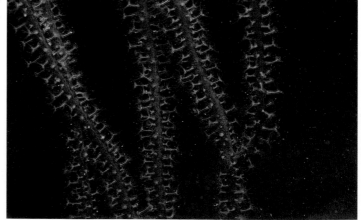

COLORFUL SEA WHIP
Leptogorgia virgulata
SUBORDER:
Holaxonia
FAMILY:
Gorgoniidae

SIZE: Colony height
¹/₂ - 1 ¹/₂ ft.
DEPTH: 25 - 130 ft.

Colorful Sea Whip
Violet variation.

Gorgonians

VISUAL ID: Colonies thickly branched, generally in single planes. Branches somewhat flattened. Polyps alternate in rows along edges. Rows are separated by distinct grooves on older main branches. Calyces generally more prominent in older parts of colony. Branches orange to red, reddish purple and purple; polyps translucent to white.

ABUNDANCE & DISTRIBUTION: Common both coasts of Florida. Not known from Bahamas, Caribbean.

HABITAT & BEHAVIOR: Inhabit most environments, especially in areas with hard substrate and some sand.

NOTE: Small sample of pictured specimen was collected and visual identification confirmed by microscopic examination of spicules. Formerly classified in genus *Lophogorgia*, which is no longer considered valid.

Regal Sea Fan
Branch detail with polyps extended.

VISUAL ID: Small openly pinnate branching colonies. Commonly branch in a single plane, but may be somewhat bushy. Low blunt calyces form a single rows along each edge of outer branches; thicker branches have double rows. Branches orange-red to red to reddish purple; polyps translucent white.

ABUNDANCE & DISTRIBUTION: Occasional Florida, southeastern and southern Caribbean. Not reported Bahamas or remainder of Caribbean.

HABITAT & BEHAVIOR: Inhabit most environments, especially in areas with hard substrate and some sand.

NOTE: Small sample of pictured specimen was collected and visual identification confirmed by microscopic examination of spicules. Formerly classified in genus *Lophogorgia*, which is no longer considered valid.

REGAL SEA FAN
Leptogorgia hebes
SUBORDER:
Holaxonia
FAMILY:
Gorgoniidae

SIZE: Colony height
$^{1}/_{2}$ - $1^{1}/_{2}$ ft.
DEPTH: 25 - 130 ft.

Regal Sea Fan
*Branch detail with
polyps retracted.*

CARMINE SEA SPRAY
Leptogorgia miniata
SUBORDER:
Holaxonia
FAMILY:
Gorgoniidae

SIZE: Colony height
2 - 5 in.
DEPTH: 40 - 120 ft.

continued next page

Gorgonians

Carmine Sea Spray

Branch detail with polyps extended.

VISUAL ID: Fan-shaped colonies with regular pinnate branching in a single plane. Branches stiff, widely spaced and somewhat enlarged at the tips. Hard rough, prickly calyces without terminal spikes are openly spaced and protrude noticeably. Branches brownish yellow to brownish orange to orange or red; polyps' tentacles translucent to white, centers yellowish to orange or red.

ABUNDANCE & DISTRIBUTION: Occasional both Florida coasts. Not reported Bahamas, Caribbean.

HABITAT & BEHAVIOR: Inhabit clear water of moderate to deep fore reefs.

SIMILAR SPECIES: Five additional species of *Muricea* are described on pages 49-53.

NOTE: Small sample of pictured specimen was collected and visual identification confirmed by microscopic examination of spicules.

Pinnate Spiny Sea Fan

Polyp detail.

Carmine Sea Spray
*continued from
previous page*

Bushy colony.

**PINNATE SPINY
SEA FAN**
Muricea pendula
SUBORDER:
Holaxonia
FAMILY:
Plexauridae

SIZE: Colony height
8 - 18 in.
DEPTH: 40 - 120 ft.

**Pinnate Spiny
Sea Fan**
Branch detail.

Gorgonians

VISUAL ID: Lateral branching colonies generally in a single plane; larger colonies tend to be somewhat bushy. Branches of living specimens are yellow-brown to reddish brown to grayish red. Normally extended polyps bright red to pink, often with white centers.

ABUNDANCE & DISTRIBUTION: Common off Northeast Florida. Additional distribution within safe diving limits not reported. Deep dwelling specimens reported from Dry Tortugas and eastern Caribbean.

HABITAT & BEHAVIOR: Inhabit areas of hard substrate.

NOTE: Samples of pictured specimens were collected and identification made by microscopic examination of spicules.

White Eye Sea Spray
Colonies with both partially and fully retracted polyps.

WHITE EYE SEA SPRAY
Thesea nivea
SUBORDER:
Holaxonia
FAMILY:
Gorgoniidae

SIZE: Colony 6 - 18 in.
DEPTH: 75 - 1200 ft.

White Eye Sea Spray
Bushy colony.

White Eye Sea Spray
Polyp detail;
note branch color.

Polyp detail;
without white centers.
[far left]

Polyp detail;
with white centers.
[left]

Gorgonians

VISUAL ID: Colonies thickly branched, generally in single planes; often fan-shaped. Polyps usually extended and protrude dramatically from relatively thin stems. Polyps bright yellow to yellow-gold; stems yellowish to tan or brown.

ABUNDANCE & DISTRIBUTION: Common Northwest Caribbean. Not reported remainder of Caribbean, Florida or Bahamas.

HABITAT & BEHAVIOR: Inhabit deep reefs, especially along drop-offs and walls. Most common in protected areas, under ledge overhangs, wall undercuts, and inside crevices in narrow canyons; occasionally exposed on reef tops.

NOTE: Small sample of pictured specimen was collected and microscopic examination confirmed visual identification. Species first described in 1990 from Brazil, between 22-100 feet. Previously unknown in Caribbean.

VISUAL ID: Colonies form rigid stalks with large prominent, white to translucent polyps. Stalks tipped with single polyp; below, secondary (daughter) polyps grow at intervals of about ³/₈ inch. Bright red to pink. Polyps usually extended. Stalks often encrusted and/or overgrown with algae, sponge and other organisms.

ABUNDANCE & DISTRIBUTION: Uncommon Bahamas, eastern Caribbean. Not reported Florida, West or Northwest Caribbean.

HABITAT & BEHAVIOR: Inhabit deep shaded areas, such as narrow canyon walls and caves. Prefer areas regularly swept with current.

NOTE: Photographed specimen was collected (USNM 1015356) and visual identification confirmed by examination with scanning electron microscope. This species' closest relative is *S. rubra* from the Indian Ocean. Previously classified in genus *Telesto*.

86

GOLDEN SEA SPRAY
Heterogorgia uatumani
SUBORDER:
Holaxonia
FAMILY:
Plexauridae

SIZE: Colony hcight
$^{1}/_{2}$ - 1 ft.
DEPTH: 75 - 150 ft.

Golden Sea Spray
Small colony.

Polyp detail.
[far left]

Fan-shaped colony.
[left]

RIGID RED TELESTO
Stereotelesto corallina
SUBORDER:
Stolonifera
FAMILY:
Clavulariidae

SIZE: Colony height
$^{3}/_{4}$ - 2 in.
DEPTH: 75 - 600 ft.

Gorgonians

VISUAL ID: Colonies form dense clusters of tangled, branching stems with large prominent white polyps. Stems tipped with single polyps; below, secondary (daughter) polyps grow in pairs or groups of three at approximately the same level. White to pale pink stalks have eight longitudinal grooves. Polyps usually extended. Stems often encrusted and/or overgrown with algae, sponge and other organisms.

ABUNDANCE & DISTRIBUTION: Occasional South Florida, Bahamas, Caribbean.

HABITAT & BEHAVIOR: Considered a fouling organism. Can be abundant in shallow, rocky areas and under docks. In deeper water common on shipwrecks — often the first octocorallian to inhabit new wrecks/artificial reefs. Uncommon on reefs and walls.

NOTE: Previously classified in the genus *Telesto*.

VISUAL ID: Colonies form clusters of branched stems with large prominent white polyps. Stems tipped with single polyp; below, secondary (daughter) polyps extend from all sides. Yellow to orange to pale red stalks have eight longitudinal grooves. Polyps usually extended. Stems often encrusted and/or overgrown with algae, sponge and other organisms.

ABUNDANCE & DISTRIBUTION: Occasional Florida's Atlantic coast from West Palm Beach northward to Carolinas. Not reported Bahamas, Caribbean.

HABITAT & BEHAVIOR: Inhabit areas of rocky outcroppings and hard rubble, also attach to wrecks.

SIMILAR SPECIES: Red Telesto, *T. sanguinea,* is bright coral red, 75-350 feet, both Florida coasts and Keys.

NOTE: Photographed specimen was collected and visual identification confirmed by microscopic examination.

WHITE TELESTO
Carijoa riisei
SUBORDER:
Stolonifera
FAMILY:
Clavulariidae

Colony encrusting shipwreck.
[far left]

Polyp detail.
[left]

SIZE: Colony height
2 - 10 in.
DEPTH: 0 - 180 ft.

ORANGE TELESTO
Telesto fruticulosa
SUBORDER:
Stolonifera
FAMILY:
Clavulariidae

SIZE: Colony height
2 - 6 in.
DEPTH: 75 - 300 ft.

VISUAL ID: Thick rubbery trunk and branches. Clusters or tufts of eight-tentacle polyps on branch tips. Embedded skeletal elements (spicules) visible in translucent trunk and branches. Pastel shades of orange to yellow, gold and pink.

ABUNDANCE & DISTRIBUTION: Rare within safe diving limits Bahamas, Caribbean. Pictured specimens were observed at 120 feet, Cay Sal Bank, Bahamas.

HABITAT & BEHAVIOR: Inhabit deep drop-offs, often under ledge overhangs, wall undercuts and other shaded areas. Soft corals have a water vascular system that allows them to inflate to feed when the current runs and deflate during slack periods

NOTE: Previously classified in the genus *Spongodes*..

Pastel Soft Coral

VISUAL ID: White to deep purple horseshoe- or kidney-shaped, leaf-like colony. A short thin stalk used as a holdfast extends from below deep indention. Polyps with eight tentacles extend from upper surface when feeding. Rows of white polyps without tentacles scattered between feeding tentacles draw in water to inflate colonies.

ABUNDANCE & DISTRIBUTION: Uncommon Gulf of Mexico and Caribbean; absent East Florida and Bahamas.

HABITAT & BEHAVIOR: Inhabit shallow sandy areas including intertidal zones where it is often buried in sand. Often bury during day; inflate to feed at night. Can bioluminesce if disturbed. If dislodged float free, often washing ashore.

PASTEL SOFT CORAL
Stereonephthya
portoricensis
ORDER:
Alcyonacea
FAMILY:
Nephtheidae

SIZE: Colony height
$^1/_2$ -1 ft.
DEPTH: 120 - 1650 ft.

MUELLER'S SEA PANSY
Renilla muelleri
ORDER:
Pennatulacea
FAMILY:
Renillidae

SIZE: Diameter 1 - 2 in.
DEPTH: 0 - 75 ft.

Gorgonians

VISUAL ID: Rose to light or dark purple water lily pad-like colony. A thick fleshy stalk used as a holdfast extends ventrally from a deep indention. Pale yellowish brown polyps with eight tentacles on upper surface extend when feeding. Rows of polyps without tentacles draw in water to inflate the colony; ventral surface smooth.

ABUNDANCE & DISTRIBUTION: Uncommon East Florida, Caribbean.

HABITAT & BEHAVIOR: Inhabit shallow sandy areas including intertidal zones where it is often buried in sand. Inflating stalk forces colony above surface. Often bury during day; extend polyps to feed at night. Can bioluminesce if disturbed. If dislodged float free, often washing ashore.

VISUAL ID: Feather-like structures emerge from sand or mud. These colonial animals have two basic parts: a buried muscular peduncle that acts as a holdfast anchoring the colony to the bottom; a central stalk with either branch-like or leaf-like structures extending in a single plane. The side structures bear numerous feeding polyps with eight tentacles. Some colonies are thin and tall with narrow central stalks; others are more robust with thick central stalks and petal-like side branches. Colors vary. Although many species have distinctive shapes and colors their living appearances have never been matched with microscopic examination of spicules (skeletal elements) to substantiate visual identifications. Regrettably, at the time of this writing there are no taxonomic biologists working with this order in the Tropical Western Atlantic.

ABUNDANCE & DISTRIBUTION: Uncommon Florida, Bahamas, Caribbean.

HABITAT & BEHAVIOR: Often in areas with current where the polyps catch floating particles of food. Most species extend their bodies by hydrostatic pressure to feed at night. Water is drawn in or discharged through pores in small non-feeding polyps located between the larger feeding polyps.

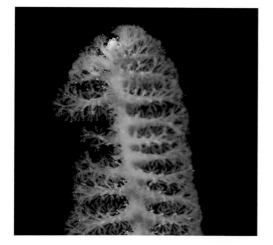

COMMON SEA PANSY
Renilla reniformis
ORDER:
Pennatulacea
FAMILY:
Renillidae

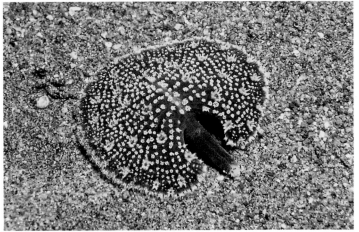

SIZE: Diameter 1 - 2 in.
DEPTH: 0 - 25 ft.

FEATHER SEA PENS
Unidentified
ORDER:
Pennatulacea
FAMILY:
Vigulariidae
Pennatulidae

SIZE: Photographed
specimen 2 ft. tall

Feather Sea Pen
*Unidentified species
photographed in 20 feet
of water in Tobago.*

Feather Sea Pen
Detail. [left]

Class Anthozoa

Subclass Hexacorallia

(Hex-ah-core-AL-ee-uh/Gr. & L. six and coral animal)

Hexacorallian polyps are generally smooth and tubular with tentacles in multiples of six. The subclass has six orders that separate anemones, zoanthids, corallimorphs, tube-dwelling anemones (see *Reef Creature Identification),* black corals (see Identification Group 4), and stony corals.

Stony Corals

ORDER: Scleractinia (Scler-ak-TIN-ee-uh / L. & Gr. hard and ray)

Stony corals, often called hard corals, are the basic building blocks of tropical coral reefs. These animals (polyps) secrete calcium carbonate to form hard cups, called **corallites,** that provide protection for their soft delicate bodies. In tropical waters most species grow colonially, joining their corallites to produce a substantial structure. Colonies increase in size by asexual budding of additional polyps and successive generations overgrowing one another. The maximum size, shape and design of these structures vary from species to species. Many species can be identified by simply observing the overall structure. Other species, however, grow in similar patterns and require a closer, more detailed inspection of the individual corallites or other parts of the structure before a positive species identification can be made.

Colonial corals that contribute substantial amounts of calcium carbonate (limestone) to the reef structure, are called **hermatypic** or reef-building corals. They live within a narrow temperature range, generally between 70 and 85 degrees Fahrenheit, although most species will survive for short periods, and a few hearty species will grow, in temperatures from 61 to 97 degrees. Non-reef-building corals, called **ahermatypic,** are usually small, occasionally solitary and without substantial skeletons.

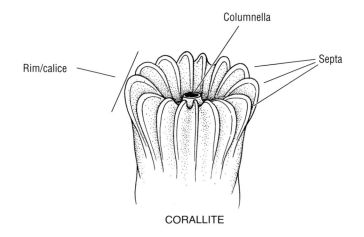

CORALLITE

To assist in the visual identification of stony corals, the 66 species identified in this text have been arranged by the shape and/or appearance of the colony, rather than the traditional scientific family groupings. This method has, in most cases, kept members of the same genus together. The groupings are: (1) **Branching & Pillar Corals**; (2) **Encrusting, Mound & Boulder Corals**; (3) **Brain Corals**; (4) **Leaf, Plate & Sheet Corals**; (5) **Fleshy Corals**; (6) **Cup & Flower Corals**.

BRANCHING & PILLAR CORALS

ENCRUSTING, MOUND & BOULDER CORALS

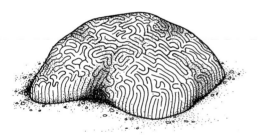

BRAIN CORALS

LEAF, PLATE & SHEET CORALS

FLESHY CORALS

FLOWERING & CUP CORALS

The shape and size of corallites are unique and distinguish species. When colonial structures are similar, close examination of the corallites' structural parts may be required before a correct identification can be made. Generally **corallites** are constructed in a circular pattern, but occasionally they are uneven, oval, Y-shaped or join to form elongated **valleys** and **ridges.** The tubular structure of the polyp's body has a number of vertical infolds on the surface. Calcium carbonate deposited in these folds form thin, upright, radiating plates or ridges, called **septa.** Often the number and structure of the septa are distinctive of species. The corallite structures of many species project above the overall colony forming distinctive rims, called **calyces,** which can also be indicative of species. The central axis of a corallite called the **columnella** is below the **polyp mouth.**

The polyps of most Caribbean stony corals are usually retracted into their corallites during the day. At night they extend both their bodies and tentacles for feeding, giving the colony a dramatically different appearance. Their nocturnal form, however, is not useful in determining species. Consequently, only occasional pictures of a coral's nighttime appearance are included in this text.

Reef building corals (hermatypic) typically get their color from single-celled algae, called **zooxanthellae** (zo-zan-THEL-ee), that live in the polyp's tissues. This symbiotic relationship is not fully understood, but clearly the biological processes of each are useful to the other. Most importantly, the zooxanthellae seem to stimulate or aid the secretion of calcium carbonate. Without the algae, coral growth slows dramatically and the polyps' tissues are transparent to translucent revealing the white calcium carbonate skeleton beneath. What causes the algae to be expelled from the polyps' tissues is currently a matter of great scientific concern and debate. It is known that this process, called bleaching, takes place during times of stress; for example, after hurricanes and when water temperatures are unusually high. When conditions return to normal, corals that are bleached regain their zooxanthellae. However, corals cannot live for prolonged periods without the algae. Continued stressful conditions are therefore cause for apprehension. The current fear is that global warming is causing the abnormally high incidence of bleaching and that this may ultimately affect the diversity of corals found on reefs. Non-reef-building corals (ahermatypic) may or may not have zooxanthellae, in which case pigments of their own become prominent. Orange Cup Coral is an example.

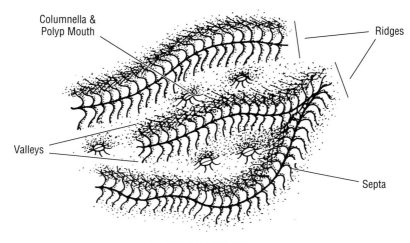

RIDGE-VALLEY

Branching & Pillar Corals

VISUAL ID: Colonies form antler-like racks of cylindrical branches that often grow in great tangles. Surface covered with small protruding, tubular corallites. Brown to yellow-brown with a single white terminal corallite. Fragile.

ABUNDANCE & DISTRIBUTION: Occasional to common Bahamas, Caribbean; occasional to uncommon South Florida. Once abundant in many locations throughout the region, but has suffered mass mortality since the early 1990's in many areas due to White-band Disease [pg. 232].

HABITAT & BEHAVIOR: Prefer shallow to intermediate depths between 10-60 feet in clear, calm water. Most commonly on reefs, but colonies may grow separately on open areas of sand. Often form dense thickets with only outer branches living; the dead interior branches are usually encrusted with algae. Rapidly growing coral; under optimum conditions can grow five to six inches per year. Polyps usually retracted during day.

Staghorn Coral
Small colony mixed with other corals.

STAGHORN CORAL
Acropora cervicornis
ORDER:
Scleractinia
FAMILY:
Acroporidae

SIZE: Colony 1 - 8 ft.
Branch diameter ³/₄ - 1¹/₄ in.
DEPTH: 1 - 160 ft.

Staghorn Coral
*Colonies may cover
large areas.*

Corallite detail.
[far left]

*Tangled colony
over sand.*
[left]

Staghorn Coral
*Huge number of colonies
covering nearly an acre of
bottom. It is doubtful
assemblages of colonies this
size still exist.*

Branching & Pillar Corals

VISUAL ID: Colonies form flattened branches resembling the horns of moose or elk. Surface covered with small protruding, tubular corallites. Brown to yellow-brown. White terminal corallites give the edges of outer branches a white outline. Somewhat fragile, branches break if pressure is applied.

ABUNDANCE & DISTRIBUTION: Common to occasional Bahamas, Caribbean. Once abundant in Florida Keys, but now only occasional and scattered. Once abundant in many locations throughout the region, but has suffered mass mortality since the early 1990's in most areas due to White-band Disease [pg. 232].

HABITAT & BEHAVIOR: Prefer shallow areas where wave action causes constant water movement. Most common between 1-35 feet. Branches orient parallel to surge direction. Can cover acres of shallow bottom. One of the primary corals of shallow fringing reefs. Upper branches may become exposed at low tide. Rapidly growing coral, under optimum conditions can grow five to six inches per year. Polyps usually retracted during day.

Elkhorn Coral
Corallite detail.

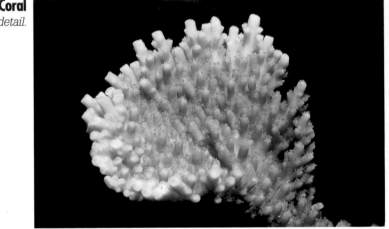

Elkhorn Coral
Colonies growing in shallow unprotected waters, especially on the windward side of fringing reefs, tend to develop rounded stout branches to withstand the force of waves and surge.

ELKHORN CORAL
Acropora palmata

ORDER:
Scleractinia
FAMILY:
Acroporidae

Colonies inhabiting moderate depths tend to develop long, wide flattened branches.

SIZE: Colony 3 - 12 ft.
Branch diameter 2 - 10 in.
DEPTH: 1 - 55 ft.

Elkhorn Coral
Colonies growing in the shallow protected lee sides of fringing reefs.

Branching & Pillar Corals

VISUAL ID: Hybridization between Staghorn Coral, *Acropora cervicornis,* and Elkhorn Coral, *A. palmata,* [previous pages]. Distinguished from parent species by numerous tightly clustered branches. Colonies are highly variable in growth pattern and appearance. Brown to yellow-brown. Surface covered with small protruding corallites and a single white terminal corallite. Fragile.

ABUNDANCE & DISTRIBUTION: Uncommon South Florida, Bahamas, Caribbean; can be locally abundant.

HABITAT & BEHAVIOR: Prefer areas of surge; fore reefs between 3-20 feet. Rapidly growing coral; under optimum conditions can grow five to six inches per year. Polyps often retracted during day.

NOTE: Based on the molecular signature, colonies of Fused Staghorn, *A. prolifera,* have not been found to reproduce with each other to form a second hybrid generation; however, molecular evidence of introgression suggest they can mate with the parental species, *A. cervicornis* and *A. palmata.* They can also reproduce asexually by fragmentation.

FUSED STAGHORN
Acropora prolifera
= A. cervicornis × palmata

ORDER:
Scleractinia
FAMILY:
Acroporidae

SIZE: Colony 1 - 12 ft.
Branch diameter ³/₄ - 6 in.
DEPTH: 1 - 90 ft.

Fused Staghorn
Colonies are highly variable in growth patterns and appearance.
[left, right & below]

VISUAL ID: Colonies of the three species in genus *Porites* form smooth branches with embedded corallites. When extended, polyps give branches a fuzzy appearance. Color ranges from beige to yellow-brown, brown, tan, and gray; uncommonly lavender to purple.

Clubtip Finger Coral, *P. porites,* branches stout, irregular and stubby with blunt and often enlarged tips. **Branched Finger Coral,** *P. furcata,* finger-like branches form compact colonies; occasionally divide near tip. **Thin Finger Coral,** *P. divaricata,* thin finger-like branches widely spaced; often divide near tip.

ABUNDANCE & DISTRIBUTION: Abundant to common South Florida, Bahamas, Caribbean.

HABITAT & BEHAVIOR: All three morphotypes inhabit most reef environments and depths.

Clubtip Finger Coral: Most common on moderate to deep reefs. **Branched Finger Coral:** Frequently form large beds on shallow back reefs and reef tops. **Thin Finger Coral:** Most common on shallow back reefs including seagrass beds and rubble areas.

NOTE: These three species were described in the late 18th and early 19th Century. However, in the late 20th Century similarities in corallite structures and general appearance of the corallites have prompted many coral scientists to speculate that there is only a single branching species of *Porites* in the Caribbean. A consensus has yet to be reached.

Thin Finger Coral
Lavender variation.

CLUBTIP FINGER CORAL
Porites porites
ORDER:
Scleractinia
FAMILY:
Poritidae

SIZE: Colony 1 - 4 ft.
Branch diameter 1 - 1¹/₂ in.
DEPTH: 3 - 160 ft.

BRANCHING FINGER CORAL
Porites furcata
ORDER:
Scleractinia
FAMILY:
Poritidae

SIZE: Colony 1 - 6 ft.
Branch diameter ³/₄ - 1¹/₄ in.
DEPTH: 3 - 160 ft.

THIN FINGER CORAL
Porites divaricata
ORDER:
Scleractinia
FAMILY:
Poritidae

SIZE: Colony 1 - 2 ft.
Branch diameter ¹/₄ - 1 in.
DEPTH: 3 - 160 ft.

VISUAL ID: Colonies form numerous heavy, cylindrical spires that grow upward from an encrusting base. Light tan to golden brown and chocolate brown. (Similar Whitevalley Maze Coral, *Meandrina jacksoni,* [pg. 151] has an unusual growth pattern variation that appears somewhat structurally similar, but the septa pattern of upright plates and ridge grooves is distinctive.)

ABUNDANCE & DISTRIBUTION: Occasional to rare South Florida, Bahamas, Caribbean.

HABITAT & BEHAVIOR: Inhabit flat and gently sloping bottoms. Polyps are normally extended during the day giving colonies a fuzzy appearance. Fallen pillars often give rise to several new upward growing pillars.

Pillar Coral
Extended polyp detail.

PILLAR CORAL
Dendrogyra cylindrus

ORDER:
Scleractinia
FAMILY:
Meandrinidae

SIZE: Colony 4 - 10 ft.
Pillar diameter 3 - 5 in.
DEPTH: 4 - 65 ft.

Pillar Coral
*Fallen colony growing
new upright pillars.*

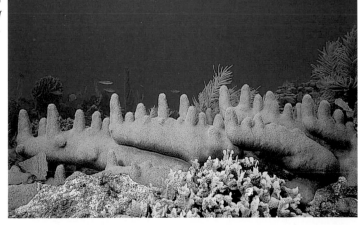

Mature colony.
[far left]

Young colony.
[left]

107

Branching & Pillar Corals

VISUAL ID: Colonies form large, bushy or tree-like structures. Colony base (trunk) can be quite thick, branches long and tapering. Only corallites' rims protrude from colony. (Similar Large Ivory Coral, *Oculina varicosa*, Delicate Ivory Bush Coral, *O. tenella*, and Diffuse Ivory Bush Coral, *O. diffusa*, [next three species] distinguished by prominently protruding corallites.) Yellowish brown. Thin branch tips fragile.

ABUNDANCE & DISTRIBUTION: Abundant West Florida. Absent East Florida, Bahamas, Caribbean.

HABITAT & BEHAVIOR: Inhabit areas of hard substrate.

NOTE: Photographed specimen collected and visual identification confirmed by magnified examination of corallites and structure.

VISUAL ID: Colonies form large tangled clumps of long crooked branches. Corallites extend prominently from raised mounds on branches' sides, except on smaller branches and near branch tips. Yellowish brown; without zooxanthellae, white to lavender. Thinner branches fragile.

ABUNDANCE & DISTRIBUTION: Uncommon Florida; rare to absent Bahamas, Caribbean.

HABITAT & BEHAVIOR: Wide range of habitats from shallow reefs to deep, rocky outcroppings. Rare in shallow water, most common between 150-300 feet; small colonies not uncommon between 75-125 feet along central and northern Atlantic Coast of Florida.

NOTE: Photographed specimens collected (USNM 91669); visual identification confirmed by magnified examination of corallites and structure.

Large Ivory Coral
Small colony.

(USNM 91670)

ROBUST IVORY TREE CORAL
Oculina robusta
ORDER:
Scleractinia
FAMILY:
Oculinidae

SIZE: Colony 4 - 30 in.
Corallite diameter to ¹/₄ in.
Branch diameter to 3 in.
DEPTH: 20 - 85 ft.

LARGE IVORY CORAL
Oculina varicosa
ORDER:
Scleractinia
FAMILY:
Oculinidae

SIZE: Colony 3 - 24 in.
Corallite diameter ¹/₄ in.
Branch diameter ¹/₂ - 2 in.
DEPTH: 15 - 300 ft.

Large Ivory Coral
*Branch detail;
note corallites'
swollen bases.*

Branching & Pillar Corals

VISUAL ID: Colonies form small clumps of thin branches. Branches may occasionally cross and fuse. Corallites protrude prominently from sides of branches. Branch diameter, corallite diameter and length all nearly equal. Cream to white. Fragile. Ahermatypic and often without zooxanthellae.

ABUNDANCE & DISTRIBUTION: Uncommon West Florida; rare East Florida. Not reported Bahamas, Caribbean.

HABITAT & BEHAVIOR: Inhabit areas of rocky rubble, shell hash, beneath ledge overhangs and on shipwrecks.

NOTE: Photographed specimen collected (USNM 91649); visual identification confirmed by magnified examination of corallites and structure.

VISUAL ID: Colonies form densely branched, thicket-like clumps. Branches tend to be short, often crooked, and bear numerous raised corallites. Yellow-brown, but often encrusted with organisms of different color. Somewhat fragile and may lack zooxanthellae.

ABUNDANCE & DISTRIBUTION: Abundant to occasional Florida; common to occasional Bahamas; occasional to rare Caribbean. Absent around some islands, especially in northwest and southern Caribbean.

HABITAT & BEHAVIOR: Generally inhabit shallow water areas of high sedimentation, including sloping solid bottoms, reefs, back reefs and lagoons. Often attach to old shipwrecks. Much of the colonies are often dead, and covered with sediment. Rarely below 40 feet.

SIMILAR SPECIES: Ivory Tree Coral, *Oculina valenciennesi,* distinguished by longer, more tree-like branches, corallite rims low and often sunken into the branch structure. Common Bermuda; rare or absent Florida, Bahamas, Caribbean.

Diffuse Ivory Bush Coral
Colony with some branches lacking zooxanthellae and others with lavender pigmentation.

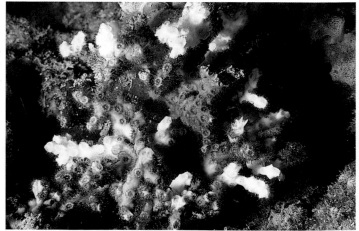

110

DELICATE IVORY BUSH CORAL
Oculina tenella

ORDER:
Scleractinia
FAMILY:
Oculinidae

SIZE: Colony 1 - 4 in.
Corallite diameter $1/8$ in.
Branch diameter to $1/4$ in.
DEPTH: 60 - 250 ft.

DIFFUSE IVORY BUSH CORAL
Oculina diffusa

ORDER:
Scleractinia
FAMILY:
Oculinidae

SIZE: Colony 1 - 12 in.
Corallite diameter $1/4$ in.
Branch diameter to $1/2$ in.
DEPTH: 3 - 75 ft.

Diffuse Ivory Bush Coral

Colony on dark interior ceiling of shipwreck lacks zooxanthellae.

(USNM 92075)

VISUAL ID: Colonies form small densely branching clumps in shallow water. In depths below 65 feet branches becomes more widely spaced. Branches have fine ridges running their length, and each ends with a single corallite. Tan to golden brown and dark brown. Fragile.

ABUNDANCE & DISTRIBUTION: Common to occasional Florida, Bahamas, Caribbean.

HABITAT & BEHAVIOR: Most commonly inhabit shallow areas with heavy sedimentation, such as Turtle Grass beds. Rarely on clear water reefs. Much of the colonies are often dead and covered with sediment, with only polyps at tips of outer branches living.

NOTE: Also commonly known as Ivory Tube Coral. Formerly classified in family Caryophylliidae.

VISUAL ID: Colonies form densely packed clumps of small pencil-sized branches with blunt tips. Colonies appear fuzzy when polyps are extended. Creamy to bright yellow. Fragile.

ABUNDANCE & DISTRIBUTION: Common South Florida, Bahamas, Caribbean.

HABITAT & BEHAVIOR: Generally inhabit deeper, clear water, outer reefs. Occasionally in shallower water with some sedimentation and water movement. Often cover considerable area of flat bottom. Polyps are generally extended.

SIMILAR SPECIES: Pointed Pencil Coral, *M. asperula,* branches tapered rather than blunt. A deep dwelling azooxanthellate coral known primarily from the southern Caribbean.

NOTE: Also commonly known as Small Finger Coral and Branching Coral. Formerly classified as *mirabilis.*

Yellow Pencil Coral

Small colony with polyps extended.

TUBE CORAL
Cladocora arbuscula
ORDER:
Scleractinia
FAMILY:
Oculinidae

SIZE: Colony 1 - 6 in.
Corallite diameter ¼ in.
DEPTH: 3 - 65 ft.

YELLOW PENCIL CORAL
Madracis auretenra
ORDER:
Scleractinia
FAMILY:
Pocilloporidae

SIZE: Colony 5 in. - 4 ft.
Branch diameter ¼ - ⅜ in.
DEPTH: 3 - 190 ft.

Yellow Pencil Coral
Branch detail;
note blunt tips.

Branching & Pillar Corals

VISUAL ID: Colonies form columns that occasionally branch and often have bluntly rounded or expanded double-lobed tips. Columns are somewhat irregular rather than perfectly round and often have flattened sides. Corallites have eight septa (rays) and are widely separated (compare similar Ten-ray Finger Coral, *Madracis carmabi*, [next] and Ten-ray Star Coral, *M. decactis*, [next page] have corallites with ten septa that are more tightly compacted). Usually yellow brown to brown to red brown, occasionally with green tint. Polyp mouths yellow to chartreuse.

ABUNDANCE & DISTRIBUTION: Uncommon to rare South Florida, Bahamas, Caribbean; also Gulf of Mexico.

HABITAT & BEHAVIOR: Inhabit deep outer reefs and slopes protected from wave action; often on outcroppings and ledges along walls. Rarely shallower than 90 feet, most common below 110 feet.

NOTE: Also commonly known as Branching Cactus Coral.

VISUAL ID: Colonies form thick, compact, columnar branches with bluntly rounded or lobed tops. Branches tipped with two or three lobes tend to grow in a single uneven or lumpy plane. Corallites have ten septa (rays) and are somewhat compact (compare similar Eight-ray Finger Coral, *Madracis formosa*, [above] with widely separated corallites with eight septa). Branches are shades of brown, but colonies commonly appear green with yellowish columnar tops because the greenish yellow polyps are often expanded masking the underlying color.

ABUNDANCE & DISTRIBUTION: Uncommon to rare South Florida, Bahamas, Caribbean.

HABITAT & BEHAVIOR: Inhabit mid-range reefs and slopes protected from wave action, often on outcroppings and ledges along walls. Rarely shallower than 70 feet or deeper than 130 feet.

NOTE: Many coral scientists believe this species is a hybrid between Eight-ray Finger Coral and Ten-ray Star Coral, *M. decactis*, or Star Coral, *M. pharensis*, [following pages] by a process following the principles of reticulate evolution.

EIGHT-RAY FINGER CORAL
Madracis formosa
ORDER:
Scleractinia
FAMILY:
Pocilloporidae

SIZE: Colony 1 - 5 ft.
Branch diameter ³/₄ - 1¹/₄ in.
DEPTH: 60 -180 ft.

Eight-ray Finger Coral
Note the wide spacing between corallites and the eight septa (compared to Ten-ray Finger Coral). [next]

TEN-RAY FINGER CORAL
Madracis carmabi
ORDER:
Scleractinia
FAMILY:
Pocilloporidae

SIZE: Colony 1 - 5 ft.
Branch diameter ³/₄ - 1¹/₄ in.
DEPTH: 60 -135 ft.

Encrusting, Mound & Boulder Corals

VISUAL ID: Small, thin encrusting colonies often with raised, tightly bunched lobes or knobs. Surface densely covered with small, separated, protruding corallites with ten septa (rays). Often green, but vary from yellow-brown to violet-brown, tan and gray.

ABUNDANCE & DISTRIBUTION: Common South Florida, Bahamas, Caribbean.

HABITAT & BEHAVIOR: Inhabit most reef environments. Usually develop lobes and knobs when growing in the open and exposed to bright light. Form irregular encrustations in shaded, protected areas of reef, under ledge overhangs and on deep walls.

NOTE: Encrusting variation is visually indistinguishable from Encrusting Star Coral, *Madracis pharensis* form *luciphila*, [next page], but can usually be identified by habitat. Positive identification requires magnified examination of specimen sample. Ten-ray Star Coral has ten primary septa, while Encrusting Star Coral has ten primary and ten secondary septa and small lobes around the columella. Identification of pictured specimens was confirmed by examination of small collected samples.

Six-ray Star Coral
Large encrusting colony on deep wall.

VISUAL ID: Thick encrusting colonies generally conform to the contours of the substrate. Cylindrical corallites are closely spaced and noticeably larger that those of similar appearing species in the genus. Readily distinguished by its six septa around the edge of the corallite that extend well above the cup structure as rounded lobes. Green to chocolate brown.

ABUNDANCE & DISTRIBUTION: Occasional Bahamas, Caribbean.

HABITAT & BEHAVIOR: Inhabit most deep reef environments, most common below 70 feet.

TEN-RAY STAR CORAL
Madracis decactis
ORDER:
Scleractinia
FAMILY:
Pocilloporidae

SIZE. Colony 4 - 39 in.
Lobe diameter 1 in.
DEPTH: 5 - 130 ft.

Ten-ray Star Coral
Corallite detail; knobby
and encrusting variation.

SIX-RAY STAR CORAL
Madracis senaria
ORDER:
Scleractinia
FAMILY:
Pocilloporidae

SIZE: Colony 1 - 2 ft.
DEPTH: 50 - 130 ft.

Encrusting, Mound & Boulder Corals

VISUAL ID: Colonies grow in two forms. Form *pharensis* [right] is either thinly encrusting, spreading in long ribbons, or may form numerous small knobs. May be shades of cream, yellow, pale green, dull red, pink or lavender. Ahermatypic. Form *luciphila* is thickly encrusting and may have a smooth or somewhat lumpy surface. Green to brown or gray. Hermatypic.

ABUNDANCE & DISTRIBUTION: Occasional Bahamas, Caribbean. Not reported Florida.

HABITAT & BEHAVIOR: Form *pharensis* grows in dark areas, such as the underside of plate corals and cave ceilings; most common below 60 feet. Form *luciphila* generally grows in exposed, well lighted areas of reef, often encrusting the faces of cliffs, canyon and drop-offs; may exist as shallow as six feet.

NOTE: Form *luciphila* is visually indistinguishable from the encrusting variation of Ten-ray Star Coral, *Madracis decactis*, [see previous note]. There is evidence suggesting that Encrusting Star Coral is a form of Ten-ray Star Coral. (See D. Fenner, *Bull.Mar.Sci.*, Vol. 53, No. 3, 1993.) Identification confirmed by examination of collected samples.

VISUAL ID: Colonies form thin plates that encrust and contour over the substrate, occasionally with lumpy surfaces. Colonies' edges extending outward from substrate are often undulated and generally rounded. May form overlapping, shingle-like plates. Colonies brown to reddish brown; polyps deep red-brown with brightly contrasting pale green centers that distinguish them from similar appearing coral colonies.

ABUNDANCE & DISTRIBUTION: Uncommon Central American coast and offshore islands from Colombia to Yucatan. Possibly a much wider distribution.

HABITAT & BEHAVIOR: Inhabit sloping reef faces, attaching to and encrusting the rocky substrate; also reported to overgrow sponges and areas of algae.

NOTE: This species was first described in 1990; its distribution and abundance are not well documented.

STAR CORAL
Madracis pharensis
ORDER:
Scleractinia
FAMILY:
Pocilloporidae

Form *pharensis.*

SIZE: Colony 1 - 6 in.
DEPTH: 6 - 450 ft.

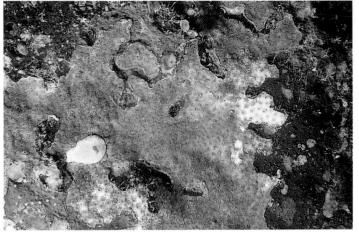

Star Coral
Form pharensis;
knobby variation
on deep cave ceiling.

Encrusting Star Coral,
form luciphila,
encrusting shallow reef.
[far left]

Encrusting shallow
canyon wall. [left]

HONEYCOMB PLATE
CORAL
Porites colonensis
ORDER:
Scleractinia
FAMILY:
Poritidae

SIZE: Colony 4 - 10 in.
DEPTH: 10 - 90 ft.

Encrusting, Mound & Boulder Corals

VISUAL ID: Colonies encrust shallow surge zones, but form rounded heads and domes in deeper water. Surface lumpy and covered with small closely set corallites that give the colonies a porous appearance. Most commonly yellow to yellow-green or yellow-brown, occasionally beige to gray. Extended polyps give colonies a soft, fuzzy appearance. A rare cryptic thin plate form that often mixes with lettuce and sheet corals can be confused with Honeycomb Plate Coral, *Porites colonensis,* [previous page].

ABUNDANCE & DISTRIBUTION: Abundant to common Florida, Bahamas, Caribbean.

HABITAT & BEHAVIOR: Inhabit most reef environments. Most common between 15-80 feet. Polyps usually extended.

NOTE: Also commonly known as Yellow Porous Coral and Porous Coral.

VISUAL ID: Colonies form thick encrustations over dead coral and rocky substrate. Extended polyps give colony soft, fuzzy appearance. When polyps are retracted, small pitted, polygonal corallites give colonies porous appearance. Pale bluish to greenish or whitish. Easily confused with Massive and Lesser Starlet Corals, *Siderastrea siderea* and *S. radians,* [next page], but can be be distinguished by color and shape of corallite pits.

ABUNDANCE & DISTRIBUTION: Occasional southern Caribbean. Not reported Florida, Bahamas and balance of Caribbean.

HABITAT & BEHAVIOR: Inhabit shallow, dead areas of older reefs. Often in back reefs with sand, coral rubble and scattered coral heads.

NOTE: An undescribed species similar to *Porites branneri* found in Brazilian waters.

MUSTARD HILL CORAL
Porites astreoides

ORDER:
Scleractinia
FAMILY:
Poritidae

SIZE: Colony 6 in. - 2 ft.
DEPTH: 3 - 160 ft.

Mustard Hill Coral

Shallow water encrusting plate growth forms; note color variations.

Polyp detail.
[far left]

Gray colony variation.
[left]

BLUE CRUST CORAL
Porites cf. branneri

ORDER:
Scleractinia
FAMILY:
Poritidae

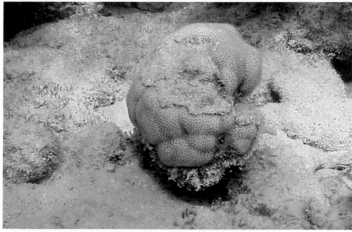

SIZE: Colony 2 - 6 in.
DEPTH: 1 - 35 ft.

Encrusting, Mound & Boulder Corals

VISUAL ID: Form rounded heads, boulders or domes. Surface covered with small, generally symmetrically round, pitted corallites. Light gray to golden-brown and brown; color uniform, corallites not dark at center. Young colonies are small, encrusting and difficult to distinguish from Lesser Starlet Coral, *Siderastrea radians*, [next] that have corallites less symmetrically round, more deeply pitted with dark centers, and more pronounced septa.

ABUNDANCE & DISTRIBUTION: Common Florida, Bahamas, Caribbean.

HABITAT & BEHAVIOR: Tend to inhabit shallow to moderate reefs between 25-45 feet. Prefer clear water. Generally grow in protected areas of shallower reefs and most deeper reef environments. Usually deeper than similar Lesser Starlet Coral.

NOTE: Also commonly known as Smooth Starlet, Round Starlet, and Reef Starlet Coral.

VISUAL ID: Colonies usually form flat encrusting plates, but occasionally grow in small irregular rounded domes. In shallow water may form unattached, egg-shaped colonies that are rolled freely across the bottom by surge. Surface is covered with small, deep-pitted corallites that often appear "pinched-in." Usually whitish to light gray, occasionally light tan; center of corallite appears dark. Can be confused with Massive Starlet Coral, *Siderastrea siderea*, [previous] that have less steeply sloping corallites, lack dark centers, and septa less pronounced; also may be confused with Blue Crust Coral, *Porites* cf. *branneri*, [previous page].

ABUNDANCE & DISTRIBUTION: Common Florida, Bahamas, Caribbean.

HABITAT & BEHAVIOR: Inhabit flat rocky/sandy substrates, most commonly from low tide line to 20 feet, also shallow reefs and back reefs. Rarely below 30 feet. Can tolerate surge, silty conditions and temperature fluctuations. Usually shallower than similar Massive Starlet Coral.

NOTE: Also commonly known as Rough Starlet, Starlet Coral, and Shallow-water Starlet Coral.

MASSIVE STARLET CORAL
Siderastrea siderea

ORDER:
Scleractinia
FAMILY:
Siderastreidae

SIZE: Colony 1 - 6 ft.
DEPTH: 2 - 220 ft.

Massive Starlet Coral

Corallite detail comparison:
Massive Starlet [left],
Lesser Starlet. [right]

Golden-brown dome colony.
[far left]

Young encrusting colonies.
[left]

LESSER STARLET CORAL
Siderastrea radians

ORDER:
Scleractinia
FAMILY:
Siderastreidae

SIZE: Colony 4 - 12 in.
DEPTH: 0 - 90 ft.

Encrusting, Mound & Boulder Corals

VISUAL ID: Colonies form relatively smooth domes or boulders; occasionally encrust substrate. Circular, upper rims of calyces darker than surrounding area. Brownish cream to tan, brown and gray. Corallites may be widely spaced or close together. When approached or touched appear to "blush" a lighter shade. (This is caused by the rapid retraction of its tiny polyps that are normally extended.)

ABUNDANCE & DISTRIBUTION: Occasional South Florida, Bahamas, Caribbean.

HABITAT & BEHAVIOR: Inhabit most reef environments. Numerous reddish Blushing Star Coral Fanworms, *Vermiliopsis* n. sp., often associate with this species. When present, they retract with the polyps, enhancing the blushing effect.

NOTE: Visual identification of pictured specimens confirmed by collection of small samples and magnified examination of corallites. Formerly classified as *michelinii*.

Blushing Star Coral
Encrusting variation;
polyps extended.

(USNM 92955)

Blushing Star Coral
Tightly compacted polyp
variation; note fanworms.

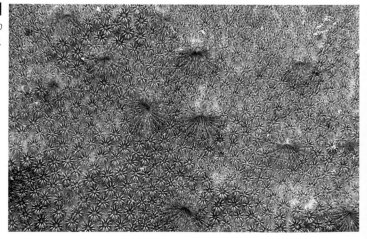

BLUSHING STAR CORAL
Stephanocoenia intersepta
ORDER:
Scleractinia
FAMILY:
Astrocoeniidae

SIZE: Colony $1/2$ - $2^{1}/_{2}$ ft.
DEPTH: 10 - 130 ft.

Blushing Star Coral
Detail: encrusting variation,
polyps retracted.

Blushing Star Coral
Boulder variation with
tightly spaced polyps.

(USNM 92954)

125

Encrusting, Mound & Boulder Corals

VISUAL ID: Colonies usually form massive boulders and domes, but occasionally develop into plates or sheets, especially in deep water. Surface is covered with large distinctive, blister-like corallites. Shades of green, brown, yellow-brown and gray. Occasionally fluoresce red or orange. (Fluorescence is not visible when lit by a hand light.)

ABUNDANCE & DISTRIBUTION: Abundant to common South Florida, Bahamas, Caribbean.

HABITAT & BEHAVIOR: Inhabit most reef environments and are often the predominant coral between 40-100 feet. Polyps are generally retracted during the day, but extend prominently at night.

NOTE: Also commonly known as Large Star Coral.

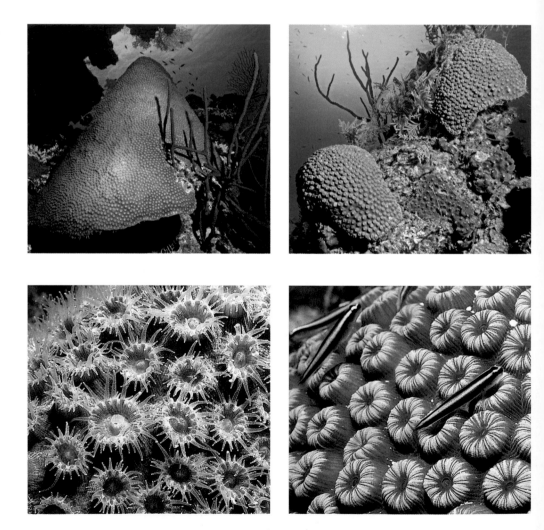

GREAT STAR CORAL
Montastraea cavernosa
ORDER:
Scleractinia
FAMILY:
Montastraeidae

SIZE: Colony 2 - 8 ft.
Corallite diameter $1/4$ - $1/2$ in.
DEPTH: 6 - 300 ft.

Great Star Coral

Polyps extended.
[far left]
Corallite detail.
[left]

Encrusting, Mound & Boulder Corals

VISUAL ID: Colonies grow in clusters of long thick columns with enlarged dome-like tops. Living polyps are restricted to the upper portions of the column, while the lower portions of columns are often bioeroded and fouled with algae or encrusting sponge. Surfaces of living coral are usually smooth with close, uniformly distributed and evenly extended corallites. Shades of green to brown, yellow-brown and gray.

ABUNDANCE & DISTRIBUTION: Abundant to common South Florida, Bahamas, Caribbean; also Gulf of Mexico.

HABITAT & BEHAVIOR: Inhabit most reef environments and along with Mountainous and Boulder Star Corals, *Orbicella faveolata* and *O. franksi,* [following pages] are often the predominate corals between 20-75 feet.

NOTE: For many years Lobed, Mountainous and Boulder Star Corals, *O. annularis, faveolata* & *franksi*, were thought to be different growth forms of a single species because of their similarity in corallite structure and called Common Star Coral, *Montastraea annularis*. In the early 1990's scientists found evidence that indicated they were three different species and not just one. Today most in the coral scientific community agree they are three closely related species. Recently the genus name *Montastraea* was changed to *Orbicella*.

Lobed Star Coral

LOBED STAR CORAL
Orbicella annularis

ORDER:
Scleractinia
FAMILY:
Merulinidae

SIZE: Colony 1 - 10 ft.
Corallite diameter ⅛ in.
DEPTH: 6 - 130 ft.

Lobed Star Coral
Unusually large colony.

Lobed Star Coral
Colonies form columnar structures, usually lower portions are dead, bio-eroded and fouled with algae or other growth, such as encrusting sponge leaving only the lobed upper tips with living polyps.
[left & right]

129

Encrusting, Mound & Boulder Corals

VISUAL ID: Colonies grow in massive mounds and large sheets with skirt-like edges. Often cone-like bumps form on the surface that are usually arranged in vertical rows. Surfaces are usually smooth with uniformly distributed and evenly extended corallites. In deep water there are two flat plate-like growth forms, the surface of some are lumpy while others are smooth; often they are stacked in shingle-like fashion. Colonies shades of green to brown, yellow-brown and gray.

ABUNDANCE & DISTRIBUTION: Abundant to common South Florida, Bahamas, Caribbean; also Gulf of Mexico.

HABITAT & BEHAVIOR: Inhabit most reef environments and along with Lobed and Boulder Star Corals, *Orbicella annularis* and *O. franksi,* [previous & following pages] are often the predominate corals between 20-75 feet, although Mountainous Star Coral is usually the most common of the three. The plate-like growth forms generally grow at depths below 80 ft.

MOUNTAINOUS STAR CORAL
Orbicella faveolata

ORDER:
Scleractinia
FAMILY:
Merulinidae

SIZE: Colony 1 - 18 ft.
Corallite diameter 1/8 in.
DEPTH: 6 - 130 ft.

Mountainous Star Coral
Typically form large mounds.
[left & right].

*Sheets with skirt-like edges
may encrust large areas of
bottom.* [far left]

Mountainous Star Coral
*Polyps extended
to feed at night.*

*Two growth forms of flattened
plates, lumpy* [far left] *and
smooth* [left] *often grow in
shingle-like fashion
below 80 feet.*

Encrusting, Mound & Boulder Corals

VISUAL ID: Colonies grow in irregular mounds and encrustations with scattered lumps. Surfaces are rough because of unevenly distributed corallites of unequal size and height. Often small clusters of polyps, especially on extended lumps, are pale to white due to lack of zooxanthellae. Colonies shades of green to brown, yellow-brown and gray.

ABUNDANCE & DISTRIBUTION: Abundant to common South Florida, Bahamas, Caribbean. Also Gulf of Mexico.

HABITAT & BEHAVIOR: Inhabit most reef environments and along with Lobed and Mountainous Star Corals, *Orbicella annularis* and *O. faveolata*, [previous pages] are often the predominate corals between 20-75 feet, although Boulder Star Coral is usually the least common of the three.

VISUAL ID: Usually form small hemispherical domes, but occasionally encrust small areas of substrate. Corallites are generally oval with protruding rims. Yellow to golden-brown and brown. (Easily distinguished from similar Elliptical Star Coral, *Dichocoenia stokesi*, [next] by colonies' smaller size and less pronounced protrusion of corallites.)

ABUNDANCE & DISTRIBUTION: Common Florida, Bahamas, Caribbean.

HABITAT & BEHAVIOR: Inhabit shallow reefs and rocky substrates. Most common between 10-40 feet.

NOTE: Also commonly known as Star Coral.

BOULDER STAR CORAL
Orbicella franksi
ORDER:
Scleractinia
FAMILY:
Merulinidae

SIZE: Colony ½ - 3 ft.
Corallite diameter ⅛ in.
DEPTH: 6 - 130 ft.

Boulder Star Coral
Corallites on surface of colonies are unevenly distributed and unequal in height and size. [right & left]

GOLFBALL CORAL
Favia fragum
ORDER:
Scleractinia
FAMILY:
Mussidae
SUBFAMILY:
Faviinae

SIZE: Colony 1 - 2 in.
DEPTH: 3 - 90 ft.

Encrusting, Mound & Boulder Corals

VISUAL ID: Colonies growth patterns are highly variable; most commonly form rounded heads or domes and flattened plates, but occasionally forms pillars, mounds with lumps and shingle-like plates. Corallites are also highly variable; some colonies have small corallites that barely project above the surface, while others protrude noticeably. The shape of corallite is also variable; most are circular to elliptical, but others are Y-shaped, worm-like or somewhat triangular. Typically shades of brown to yellow-brown or tan.

ABUNDANCE & DISTRIBUTION: Common Bahamas, Caribbean; occasional South Florida.

HABITAT & BEHAVIOR: Inhabit most reef environments, most frequently between 30-80 feet. Rarely grows on reef crests.

NOTE: The flattened plate variation was formerly known as Pancake Star Coral and classified as a separate species, *D. stellaris*, but because of the wide variety of overlapping growth patterns all variations are now considered a single species *D. stokesi*.

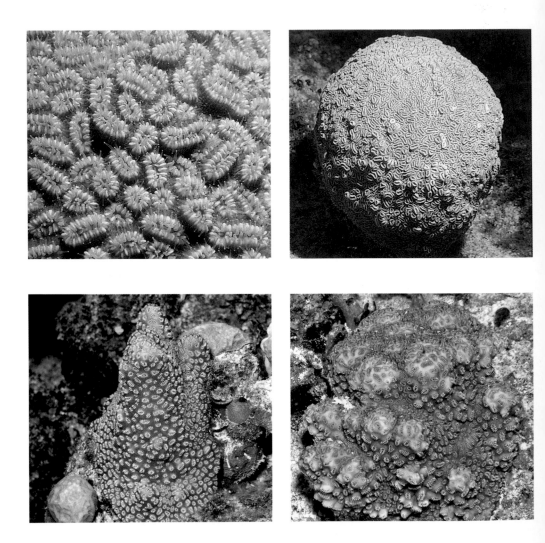

ELLIPTICAL STAR CORAL
Dichocoenia stokesii

ORDER:
Scleractinia
FAMILY:
Meandrinidae

SIZE: Colony 4 - 15 in.
DEPTH: 12 - 225 ft.

Elliptical Star Coral
Flattened plate variation.

Polyp/corallite detail.
[far left]

Rounded head variation.
[left]

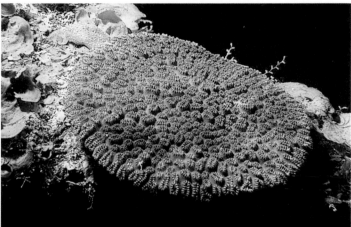

Elliptical Star Coral
Colony with unusually long, raised corallites.

Unusual pillar growth variation. [far left]

Unusual variation forming a mound with lumpy extensions. [left]

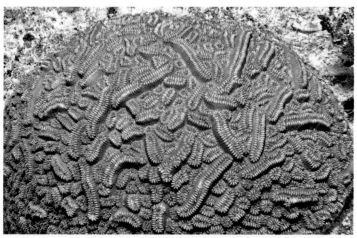

135

Encrusting, Mound & Boulder Corals

VISUAL ID: Colonies form relatively smooth domes, occasionally with a few irregular bulges and knobs on their surface. Corallite rims protrude noticeably creating a blistered appearance. Cream to light tan to greenish tan; extended polyps light tan to brown.

ABUNDANCE & DISTRIBUTION: Common to occasional South Florida; uncommon Bahamas, Caribbean; also Gulf of Mexico and the northern coast of Yucatan.

HABITAT & BEHAVIOR: Inhabit reefs from shallow to moderate depths.

VISUAL ID: Colonies form lobed heads with irregular bulges on the surface. Corallite rims protrude noticeably and are irregularly spaced, some almost touching, while others may be separated by as much as their diameter. Usually yellow-brown, occasionally cream to tan; polyps dark brown.

ABUNDANCE & DISTRIBUTION: Abundant to occasional Florida; occasional to rare Bahamas, Caribbean.

HABITAT & BEHAVIOR: Inhabit a wide range of environments from areas with heavy sedimentation, including back reefs, lagoons and Turtle Grass beds to deep outer reefs. Can tolerate cool water; grow as far north as North Carolina where winter water temperatures may fall below 50°F.

NOTE: Also commonly known as Stump Coral and Eyed Coral.

SMOOTH STAR CORAL
Solenastrea bournoni
ORDER:
Scleractinia
FAMILY:
Faviidae

SIZE: Colony 4 - 18 in.
DEPTH: 5 - 60 ft.

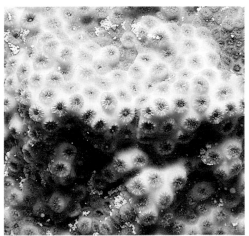

KNOBBY STAR CORAL
Solenastrea hyades
ORDER:
Scleractinia
FAMILY:
Faviidae

SIZE: Colony 3 in. - 2 ft.
DEPTH: 2 - 60 ft.

137

Brain Corals

VISUAL ID: Colonies generally form large rounded domes, but also encrust constructing large rounded plates. Surface covered with a convoluted system of ridges and valleys. A thin, but distinct, groove runs along the ridge tops. There is also a thin, but noticeable line approximately halfway down the ridge where the slope decreases its angle and slants to form the valley. Typically the ridges are brown and valleys green, tan or whitish. Valleys are usually long and meandering, containing several polyps, but are occasionally closed, holding only one or two polyps.

ABUNDANCE & DISTRIBUTION: Common South Florida, Bahamas, Caribbean.

HABITAT & BEHAVIOR: Generally inhabit reef tops and seaward reef slopes. Most common between 20-80 feet. Polyps extended only at night; tentacles form long meandering rows along the ridges (below).

NOTE: Colonies composed primarily of closed valleys with only one or occasionally two polyps are consider by some coral scientists to be a separate species Closed-valley Brain Coral, *Colpophyllia breviserialis,* while others consider the two growth patterns to be variations of the same species, Boulder Brain Coral, *C. natans.*

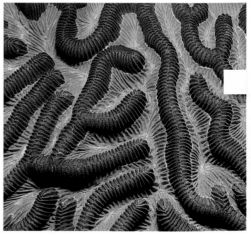

BOULDER BRAIN CORAL
Colpophyllia natans

ORDER:
Scleractinia
FAMILY:
Mussidae
SUBFAMILY:
Faviinae

SIZE: Colony 1¹/₂ - 7 ft.
DEPTH: 2 - 175 ft.

Boulder Brain Coral
Colony with closed-valleys.

*Young colony
can be confused with
Ridged Cactus Coral,*
Mycetophylia lamarckiana
pg. 167. [far left]

Closed valley form detail. [left]

Boulder Brain Coral
Massive colony.

Polyps partially extended.
[far left]

Polyps retracted.
[left]

Brain Corals

VISUAL ID: Colonies form smoothly contoured plates to hemispherical domes. Long valleys are often connected and usually convoluted, except near a colony's edge. Ridges evenly rounded, usually without a top groove, although occasionally with an extremely fine groove, especially near colony edge. (Similar Boulder Brain Coral, *Colpophyllia natans*, [previous] has a distinct groove on top of ridge. Similar Knobby Brain Coral, *Pseudodiploria clivosa*, [next] distinguished by sharply raised ridges and knobby surface.) Green to brown, yellow-brown and bluish gray; valleys often lighter or of contrasting color.

ABUNDANCE & DISTRIBUTION: Abundant to common Florida, Bahamas, Caribbean.

HABITAT & BEHAVIOR: Inhabit many marine environments, most frequently between 20-40 feet.

NOTE: Also commonly known as Common Brain Coral and Smooth Brain Coral. Formerly classified in genus *Diploria*.

SYMMETRICAL BRAIN CORAL

Pseudodiploria strigosa

ORDER:
Scleractinia
FAMILY:
Mussidae
SUBFAMILY:
Faviinae

SIZE: Colony ¹/₂ - 6 ft.
DEPTH: 3 - 130 ft.

Symmetrical Brain Coral

Hemispherical head variation.

Structural detail; note evenly rounded ridges.
[far left]

Encrusting plate variation.
[left]

Symmetrical Brain Coral

Yellowish brown variation..

Two colonies growing together to form a hemispherical dome.
[far left]

Two colonies grow together as encrusting plate.
[left]

141

Brain Corals

VISUAL ID: Colonies form hemispherical domes or encrust rocky substrate. Surfaces of colonies usually have numerous, irregular knobs, but occasionally form smooth low, flattened domes. Ridges rise sharply and occasionally display a thin groove on top, more noticeable when polyps are partly to fully expanded. (Similar Boulder Brain Coral, *Colpophyllia natans*, [pg. 139] has a distinct groove on ridge top. Similar Symmetrical Brain Coral, *Pseudodiploria strigosa*, [previous] distinguished by evenly rounded ridges and smooth contour of colonies.) Green to brown, yellow-brown and bluish gray; valleys often lighter or of contrasting color.

ABUNDANCE & DISTRIBUTION: Common Florida, Bahamas, Caribbean.

HABITAT & BEHAVIOR: Inhabit many shallow environments, including both seaward and lagoon sides of reefs, Turtle Grass beds, and mangrove roots. Most common between 3-20 feet.

NOTE: Also commonly known as Encrusting Brain Coral and Sharp-hilled Brain Coral. Formerly classified in genus *Diploria*.

Knobby Brain Coral
Encrusting plate and mounded growth forms with numerous knobs.

Knobby Brain Coral
Structural detail; note steep ridges.

KNOBBY BRAIN CORAL
Pseudodiploria clivosa

ORDER:
Scleractinia
FAMILY:
Mussidae
SUBFAMILY:
Faviinae

SIZE: Colony ½ - 4 ft.
DEPTH: 3 - 135 ft.

Knobby Brain Coral
Encrusting plate growth form.

Knobby Brain Coral
Knob with partly extended polyps, note thin groove on ridge tops.

Brain Corals

VISUAL ID: Colonies form hemispherical heads. Deep, often narrow, polyp bearing valleys are separated by broad ridges with wide, conspicuous trough-like grooves. Width and depth of grooves vary greatly from colony to colony, but are always obvious and usually make a single ridge appear as two. Valleys are highly convoluted and often interconnected. Tan to yellow-brown to brown to brownish gray.

ABUNDANCE & DISTRIBUTION: Common to occasional South Florida, Bahamas, Caribbean.

HABITAT & BEHAVIOR: Inhabit seaward slope of reefs. Most common between 15-50 feet. Tentacle tips are often visible in the narrow valleys during the day.

NOTE: Also commonly known as Depressed Brain Coral and Labyrinthine Brain Coral. Formerly classified in genus *Diploria*.

GROOVED BRAIN CORAL
Diploria labyrinthiformis

ORDER:
Scleractinia
FAMILY:
Mussidae
SUBFAMILY:
Faviinae

SIZE: Colony 1 - 4 ft.
DEPTH: 3 - 135 ft.

Grooved Brain Coral
Colony with unusually wide grooves.

Structural detail comparing different groove widths.
[left & far left]

Grooved Brain Coral
Growth variations.

Brain Corals

VISUAL ID: Colonies grow in two forms: The most common builds small elliptical colonies with long, continuous central valley and several short side valleys and cone-shaped underside, often with short central stalk. The second form builds hemispherical heads with winding valleys and ridges and flattish underside. Brown to yellow-brown, gray or green. Ridges and valleys often of contrasting shades or different colors. (Distinguished from similar appearing forms of Maze Coral, *Meandrina meandrites*, [next] by less pronounced vertical plates.) Often young colonies form small circular to oval disks that can be confused with similar appearing Solitary Disk Coral, *Scolymia wellsi*, [pg. 177].

ABUNDANCE & DISTRIBUTION: Common to uncommon Florida, Bahamas, Caribbean.

HABITAT & BEHAVIOR: The small elliptical colonies tend to inhabit areas of coral rubble, sand and Turtle Grass, and are often unattached. The hemispherical heads tend to inhabit reefs along with other stony corals, and are always attached.

NOTE: Some coral scientists consider the hemispherical head pattern a separate species or form *mayori* commonly known as Tortugas Rose Coral.

Rose Coral
Colony in Turtle Grass bed, tentacles extended.

Rose Coral
Tortugas Rose Coral form mayori *hemispherical head growth pattern.*

ROSE CORAL
Manicina areolata

ORDER:
Scleractinia
FAMILY:
Mussidae
SUBFAMILY:
Faviinae

SIZE: Elliptical
Colony 2 - 6 in.
Hemispherical
Colony 4 - 8 in.
DEPTH: 2 - 200 ft.

Rose Coral
*Tortugas Rose Coral
form* mayori;
*hemispherical head
growth pattern.*

Rose Coral
*Young disk-shaped
colony.*

(USNM 92082)

Brain Corals

VISUAL ID: Colonies form flattened plates, hemispherical heads and pillars. Ridges are created by smooth, widely separated vertical plates (septa). There is a thin line along ridge tops where plates come together. Ridges are separated by narrow deep valleys. Tan to yellow-brown and brown.

ABUNDANCE & DISTRIBUTION: Common to occasional South Florida, Bahamas, Caribbean.

HABITAT & BEHAVIOR: Inhabit most reef environments, especially on seaward reefs at depths between 25-75 feet.

NOTE: Formerly thought to have two small growth variations; form *danae* is now considered a distinct species [below] and form *brasiliensis* is now considered a distinct species known only from Brazil.

VISUAL ID: Elongate somewhat oval colonies with long central valley and usually several side valleys; often central valley divides into two branches at the ends. Mustard yellow to dark brown; sometimes with greenish tints.

ABUNDANCE & DISTRIBUTION: Occasional South Florida, Caribbean.

HABITAT & BEHAVIOR: Inhabit areas of coarse sand, algae and seagrass around reefs usually deeper than 35 feet; occasionally inhabit shallower sandy seagrass beds in water 15-30 feet. Do not attach to substrate; colonies grow a funnel-shaped projection on their anterior surface that extends into the sand to help anchor colony in place. If colony becomes dislodged and overturned, it can inflate tissue with water to right themselves.

MAZE CORAL
Meandrina meandrites
ORDER:
Scleractinia
FAMILY:
Meandrinidae

SIZE: Colony 1 - 3 ft.
DEPTH: 2 - 240 ft.

Maze Coral
Plate-like variation with polyps extended at night.

Maze Coral hemispherical head variation.
[left]

Maze Coral pillar growth variation.
[far left]

BUTTERPRINT ROSE CORAL
Meandrina danae
ORDER:
Scleractinia
FAMILY:
Meandrinidae

SIZE: Colony 2 - 6 in.
DEPTH: 15 - 100 ft.

continued next page **149**

Brain Corals

VISUAL ID: Colonies grow in a wide range of forms from simple encrustations to plates, hemispherical heads and lumpy mounds with pillar-like extensions. Low ridges are created by smooth, short vertical plates (septa), there is a thin line along ridge tops where plates come together with wide valleys between. The white tips of polyp tentacles in the valleys are typically extended. (Similar Maze Coral, *Meandrina meandrites,* [previous page] distinguished by taller ridges, wider vertical plates and narrow valleys between the ridges with polyp tentacles generally extended only at night.) Pale brown to yellow-brown, tan or uncommonly cream.

ABUNDANCE & DISTRIBUTION: Occasional South Florida, Bahamas, Caribbean.

HABITAT & BEHAVIOR: Most reef environments, especially on seaward reefs at depths between 25-75 feet, occasionally encrust shallow hard substrate.

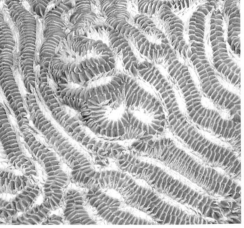

Butterprint Rose Coral

continued from previous page

Colony with a few side valleys.

Large colony, dark brown with greenish tint variation.
[far left]

Colony turned on side to show rough funnel shape that extends down into sand and does not attach to the substrate.
[left]

WHITEVALLEY MAZE CORAL

Meandrina jacksoni

ORDER:
Scleractinia
FAMILY:
Meandrinidae

SIZE: Colony ½ - 3 ft.
DEPTH: 3 - 80 ft.

White-valley Maze Coral

Flat plate-like colony.

Occasionally grow Pillar-Coral-like colony.
[far left]
Close-up showing detail.
[left]

Leaf, Plate & Sheet Corals

VISUAL ID: Colonies form thin saucers or plates with distinctive low, thin ridges (septa) that appear as lines running toward the edges; occasionally they are quite pale, contrasting dramatically with the darker underlying color. Occasionally grow in overlapping shingle-like style. Ridges and valleys are not continuous. Corallite centers are distinctively nestled in rows against ridges' steep outer edges. Inner ridge faces slope more gently toward colonies' centers. Tan to yellow-brown, brown and gray; may fluoresce green, blue or purple. Fragile.

ABUNDANCE & DISTRIBUTION: Common to occasional South Florida, Bahamas, Caribbean.

HABITAT & BEHAVIOR: Inhabit sloping reef faces and along walls. Most common between 25-100 feet.

NOTE: Also commonly known as Saucer Coral, Sunray Plate Coral, and Fragile Lettuce Coral. Formerly classified as *Leptoseris cucullata*.

Sunray Lettuce Coral
Corallite centers nestled against steep ridge edges.

Sunray Lettuce Coral
Note how the low, thin line-like ridges (septa) distinctively extend to the colonies edges.

SUNRAY LETTUCE CORAL
Helioseris cucullata
ORDER:
Scleractinia
FAMILY:
Agariciidae

SIZE: Colony 4 - 10 in.
DEPTH: 10 - 280 ft.

Sunray Lettuce Coral
Overlapping, shingle-like pattern.

Sunray Lettuce Coral
Occasionally the low, thin line-like ridges (septa) contrast dramatically with the darker underlying color of the colony.

153

Leaf, Plate & Sheet Corals

VISUAL ID: Colonies form small, thin saucer-like shapes. Ridges and long continuous valleys form an uneven pattern of concentric circles radiating from center of colonies. The ridges of deep water colonies are often low and inconspicuous. Polyps are only present in the valleys of the upper surface; the ventral surface is quite smooth. Shades of purplish brown, chocolate, yellow-brown, tan, and greenish tan. Fragile. Colonies of form *contracta* have pinched corallites and often grow in irregular, occasionally gnarled patterns.

ABUNDANCE & DISTRIBUTION: Occasional Florida, Bahamas, Caribbean.

HABITAT & BEHAVIOR: Inhabit sloping reef faces, ledge overhangs and walls.

NOTE: Visual identification of the two colonies on bottom of these pages confirmed by collection and magnified examination.

Fragile Saucer Coral
*Low profile ridges;
chocolate variation.*

Fragile Saucer Coral
*Low profile ridges;,
yellow-brown variation.*

(USNM 92094)

154

FRAGILE SAUCER CORAL
Agaricia fragilis

ORDER:
Scleractinia
FAMILY:
Agariciidae

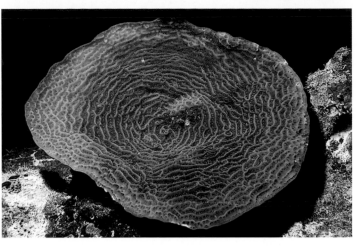

SIZE: Colony 4 - 6 in.
DEPTH: 20 - 180 ft.

Fragile Saucer Coral
Yellow-brown variation.

Fragile Saucer Coral
Constricted leaf coral form contracta;
note pinched corallites.

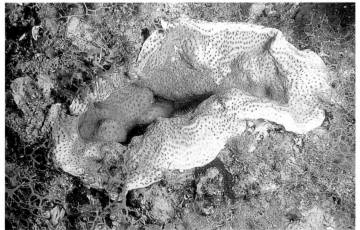

(USNM 91646)

155

Leaf, Plate & Sheet Corals

VISUAL ID: Colonies grow in massive, thin sheets or flattened plates that often form large whorls and occasionally spirals and bowls. Concentric rows of long rounded ridges and relatively wide valleys run parallel to the colonies' outer edges. Prominent, white star-like polyps in valleys' centers are distinctive of this species. Ridge ends are often tapered, rather than abruptly intersecting other ridges. Pencil-line thin septa, running between the polyp mouths, alternate in height and thickness (observation may require magnifying glass). Colonies' ventral surfaces are quite smooth and without polyps. Yellow-brown to golden-brown and brown, may have greenish, bluish or grayish tint. Fragile.

ABUNDANCE & DISTRIBUTION: Common Caribbean.

HABITAT & BEHAVIOR: Inhabit sloping reef faces and walls. One of the most abundant corals on deep reefs and walls. Most common between 65-120 feet. Massive overlapping plates often cover large areas.

NOTE: Also commonly known as Lamarck's Lettuce-leaf Coral.

Whitestar Sheet Coral
Detail: note distinctive white star-like polyps.

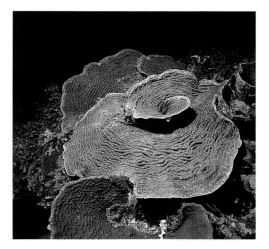

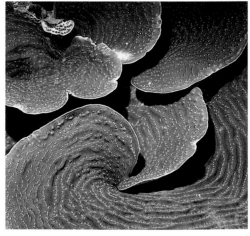

WHITESTAR SHEET CORAL
Agaricia lamarcki

ORDER:
Scleractinia
FAMILY:
Agariciidae

SIZE: Colony 1 - 6 ft.
DEPTH: 15 - 150 ft.

Whitestar Sheet Coral
Growth patterns.
[right & bottom
of both pages]

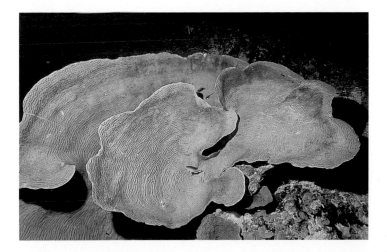

Leaf, Plate & Sheet Corals

VISUAL ID: Colonies grow rounded, thin blades that commonly curve upward in the shape of fans or bowls often creating a spiraling design. Concentric rows of long, steep sloped ridges and relatively narrow, V-shaped valleys run parallel to the colonies' pale outer edges. Pale dimple-like polyps are centered in the valleys. Pencil-line thin septa running between polyp mouths are of equal size (observation may require magnifying glass). Colonies' ventral surfaces are quite smooth and without polyps. Yellow-brown to golden-brown to brown; may have bluish, greenish or grayish tint. Fragile.

ABUNDANCE & DISTRIBUTION: Occasional Caribbean.

HABITAT & BEHAVIOR: Inhabit sloping reef faces and walls. Most common between 75-150 feet.

NOTE: Also known as Graham's Lettuce-leaf Coral and Graham's Sheet Coral.

Dimpled Sheet Coral
Bowl shaped colonies.

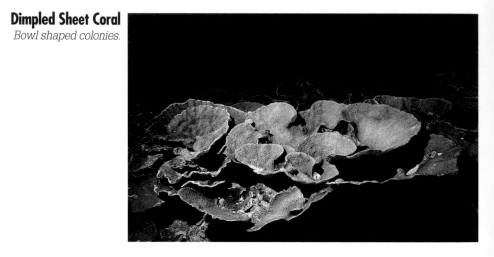

VISUAL ID: On flat and sloping substrates colonies form rounded, thin blades that curve upward forming fans or bowls. On vertical walls large spiral curving, overlapping plates may contour to the substrate. Occasionally grow in shingle-like fashion. Running around the upper surface are more-or-less continuous, wide, wavy valleys and ridges that parallel the outer edges. Corallite centers are distinctively nestled in rows against ridges' steep outer edges. Inner ridge faces slope more gently toward colonies' centers. Colonies' ventral surfaces are quite smooth and without polyps. Shades of brown to gray, often with yellowish, greenish or bluish tint; outer edge of blades often white. Fragile.

ABUNDANCE & DISTRIBUTION: Occasional Caribbean. Not reported Florida or Bahamas.

HABITAT & BEHAVIOR: Inhabit deep reefs, often on ledges or at the base of deep walls. Most common between 90-150 feet. Massive overlapping colonies occasionally cover large areas of the bottom.

DIMPLED SHEET CORAL
Agaricia grahamae
ORDER:
Scleractinia
FAMILY:
Agariciidae

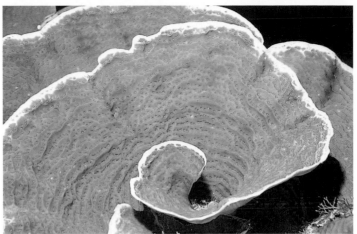

SIZE: Colony 1 - 6 ft.
DEPTH: 50 - 240 ft.

Dimpled Sheet Coral
Detail comparison: Whitestar Sheet Coral (left); note white star-like polyps and rounded ridges; Dimpled Sheet Coral (right); note long parallel valleys with steep sloped ridges.

SCROLL CORAL
Agaricia undata
ORDER:
Scleractinia
FAMILY:
Agariciidae

SIZE: Colony 1 - 6 ft.
DEPTH: 50 - 250 ft.

continued next page **159**

Leaf, Plate & Sheet Corals

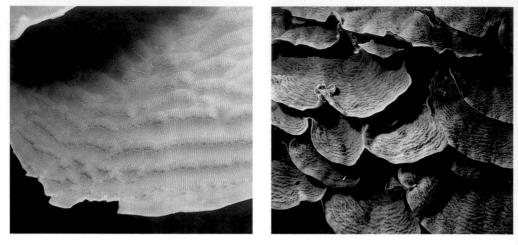

Visual Identification Key
to Similar Appearing Plate & Sheet Corals

Colonies of the following species often form structures with virtually identical shapes and sizes and often grow mixed together overlapping one another. Distinguishing the different species requires close observation of the valley and ridge structures, polyp placement and septa detail. The following guide should be helpful.

NO RIDGES OR VALLEYS

MOUNTAINOUS STAR CORAL, *Orbicella faveolata,* flattened plate growth forms [pg. 131]: small, prominently protruding, volcano-like corallites.

RIDGES AND VALLEYS, CORALLITES CENTERED IN VALLEYS

WHITESTAR SHEET CORAL, *Agaricia lamarcki,* [pg. 157]: thin, often whorled, plates. Prominent white, star-like polyps distinguish this species.

DIMPLED SHEET CORAL, *Agaricia grahamae,* [pg. 159]: thin, usually upturned plates forming fans and bowls with pale edges. Ridges rise sharply from V-shaped valleys holding dimple-like corallites.

PURPLE LETTUCE CORAL, *Agaricia agaricites* form *purpurea,* [pg. 162]: thick flat plates. Long parallel ridges and valleys mix with numerous short valleys and intersecting ridges. Ridges relatively tall and sharply raised.

RIDGES AND VALLEYS, CORALLITES NESTLED AGAINST RIDGES' OUTER EDGE

SCROLL CORAL, *Agaricia undata,* [pg. 159]: ridges are long and continuous.

SUNRAY LETTUCE CORAL, *Helioseris cucullata,* [pg. 153]: ridges tend to be short and discontinuous, septa more prominent than Scroll Coral [previous].

Scroll Coral
continued from previous page

Colony with large overlapping plates.

Detail: note corallites nestled against ridges' outer edge. [far left]

Shingle-like colonies. [left]

Mixed colonies including: Lettuce, Scroll and Whitestar Sheet Corals.

Mixed colonies including: Lettuce, Sunray Lettuce, Whitestar Sheet and Boulder Star Corals.

Leaf, Plate & Sheet Corals

VISUAL ID: Colonies grow in several forms. Form *agaricites* is thickly encrusting or hemispherical with ridges of different heights and discontinuous valleys in reticulated pattern. Form *carinata* grows in thick, flattened plates with prominent ridges and long valleys. Thick, bifacial, low, upright plates or ribbons extend from the surface. Form *purpurea* grows in thick, flat plates and is distinguished by long continuous, parallel valleys with prominent ridges. Colonies may grow in shingle-like fashion. Form *danai* grows a series of overlapping large, thick, bifacial, upright lobes. Tan to yellow-brown, grayish brown, brown and chocolate; can have bluish or purplish tint. Not especially fragile.

ABUNDANCE & DISTRIBUTION: Abundant to common Florida, Bahamas, Caribbean.

HABITAT & BEHAVIOR: Inhabit most marine environments from mangrove and back reef areas to outer reefs and walls. Form *agaricites* is the most common and generally inhabits shallow patch and back reef areas. The other forms are more common on fore reef slopes.

Lettuce Coral
Form carinata *grows in thick plates with thick bifacial upright extensions.*

Lettuce Coral
Form purpurea *grows in flat plates with long continuous, parallel valleys and tall ridges.*

LETTUCE CORAL
Agaricia agaricites
ORDER:
Scleractinia
FAMILY:
Agariciidae

SIZE: Colony 4 in. - 3 ft.
DEPTH: 3 - 240 ft.

Lettuce Coral
Form agaricites
*encrusts with
discontinuous valleys
and ridges in
reticulated patterns.*

Scaled Lettuce Coral
Form danai *grows
in series of thick,
bifacial, upright
lobes.*

Leaf, Plate & Sheet Corals

VISUAL ID: Colonies form small, generally circular, lumpy encrustations of densely packed corallites in reticulated patterns. Corallites have deep, often narrow or pinched pits. Long valleys or two-faced lobes are never present. Yellow-brown to brown or chocolate; frequently with white areas and blotches where zooxanthellae are absent.

ABUNDANCE & DISTRIBUTION: Occasional South Florida, Bahamas, Caribbean.

HABITAT & BEHAVIOR: Inhabit sloping reefs, undercuts and canyon walls. Often in somewhat protected locations. Most common between 15-35 feet.

NOTE: This species is regarded by many coral scientists as a form of Lettuce Coral, *Agaricia agaricites* form *humilis,* [previous]. Pictured specimen collected (USNM 91654) and visual identification confirmed by magnified examination.

VISUAL ID: Colonies form low clumps that resemble patches of leaf lettuce. The thin, upright blades have polyps on both sides. Wavy, parallel ridges run horizontally across the blade faces. Shades of brown to gray, often with yellowish, greenish or bluish tints. Blades fairly fragile.

ABUNDANCE & DISTRIBUTION: Abundant Northwest Caribbean, especially along Central American Coast; occasional to absent balance of Caribbean, Bahamas. Not reported Florida.

HABITAT & BEHAVIOR: Inhabit shallow reef tops, especially where wave action produces regular water movement. Numerous adjoining colonies can cover huge areas of reef tops. Most common between 15-30 feet. Narrow areas between blades provide shelter for numerous animals, including brittlestars, sea urchins and small eels. Watercress Alga often grows between the blades.

Thin Leaf Lettuce Coral

Massive colonies may cover large areas.

LOW RELIEF LETTUCE CORAL
Agaricia humilis

ORDER:
Scleractinia
FAMILY:
Agariciidae

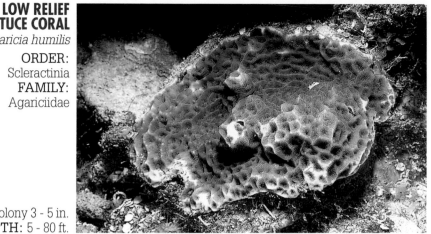

SIZE: Colony 3 - 5 in.
DEPTH: 5 - 80 ft.

THIN LEAF LETTUCE CORAL
Agaricia tenuifolia

ORDER:
Scleractinia
FAMILY:
Agariciidae

SIZE: Colony 3 - 12 ft.
DEPTH: 6 - 90 ft.

Thin Leaf Lettuce Coral
Blade detail of small colony.

Fleshy Corals

VISUAL ID: Colonies form flat plates, mounds and hemispherical domes. A ridge bordering the colony frequently grows inward and may curve, wind or even branch; may also be independent ridges on the colony. Ridge patterns and the height and depth of valleys vary according to environmental conditions. Ridges and valleys usually of contrasting colors or shades. Color variable, commonly in shades of green, brown or gray. Colonies and especially ridges may appear fleshy. Tentacles extend only from ridges.

ABUNDANCE & DISTRIBUTION: Occasional South Florida, Bahamas, Caribbean.

HABITAT & BEHAVIOR: Tend to inhabit shaded areas of shallow to moderately deep reefs, more frequently grow in the open with increasing depth. Most common between 25-75 feet. Polyps retracted during day.

NOTE: Colonies without formed ridges in the colonies' center were previously classified as a separate species, Lowridge Cactus Coral, *M. danaana.* Many scientists believe these are only young colonies that have not yet formed independent ridges or simply a growth form and should not be classified as a separate species.

Ridged Cactus Coral
Colonies without central independent ridges were formerly classified as a separate species Lowridge Cactus Coral, M. danaana.

Ridged Cactus Coral
Tentacles along edge of ridges partially extended at night

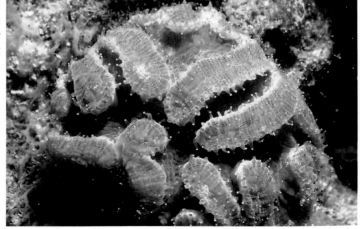

RIDGED CACTUS CORAL
Mycetophyllia lamarckiana

ORDER:
Scleractinia
FAMILY:
Mussidae
SUBFAMILY:
Mussinae

SIZE: Colony 4 - 15 in.
DEPTH: 10 - 190 ft.

Ridged Cactus Coral
Hemispherical dome growth pattern.

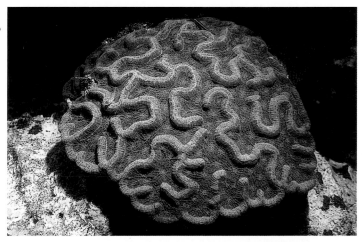

Ridged Cactus Coral
Dying colony exposing skeleton.

Fleshy Corals

VISUAL ID: Colonies thickly encrust the bottom and often overhang the edges of the substrate. A robust ridge bordering the colony frequently grows inward; short independent central ridges are also common. In deeper water the central ridges become less pronounced and occasionally disappear. Large knob-like polyp mouths in the valleys. (Similar appearing Rough Cactus Coral, *M. ferox*, [next] distinguished by small knob-like polyp mouths and less pronounced ridges.) Ridges and polyp mouths are often of light color contrasting with darker valleys in shades of green, brown, reddish or gray. Tentacles extend only from ridges.

ABUNDANCE & DISTRIBUTION: Occasional South Florida, Bahamas, Caribbean.

HABITAT & BEHAVIOR: Inhabit most moderate to deep reef environments, from patch reefs to steep slopes and walls. Most common between 40-130 feet. Polyps retracted during the day.

NOTE: Also commonly known as Thin Fungus Coral.

Knobby Cactus Coral
Protruding polyp mouths in the valleys appear as large, rounded, hill-like knobs.

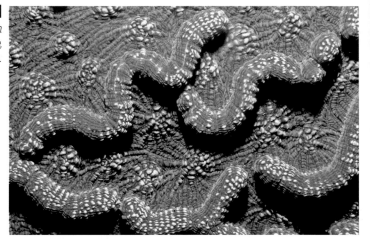

Knobby Cactus Coral
Deep water growth pattern without central ridges.

KNOBBY CACTUS CORAL
Mycetophyllia aliciae

ORDER:
Scleractinia
FAMILY:
Mussidae
SUBFAMILY:
Mussinae

SIZE: Colony 6 - 18 in.
DEPTH: 50 - 240 ft.

Knobby Cactus Coral
Young colony;
note large polyp mouths
in the wide valleys between
large rounded ridges.

Knobby Cactus Coral
Deep water colony with
moderate height ridges not
extending fully to center.

Fleshy Corals

VISUAL ID: Colonies thickly encrust the bottom and often overhang the edges of the substrate. A ridge bordering the colony frequently grows inward crisscrossing the surface often forming closed valleys and giving the colony a lattice-like appearance. In the narrow valleys are small, knob-like polyp mouths that protrude sharply. (Similar appearing Knobby Cactus Coral, *Mycetophyllia aliciae*, [previous] distinguished by large, knob-like polyp mouths and more robust ridges and wider valleys.) Ridges and polyp mouths are often of light color contrasting with darker valleys in shades of brown, pink, green, gray and bluish gray. Tentacles extend only from ridges.

ABUNDANCE & DISTRIBUTION: Occasional South Florida, Bahamas, Caribbean.

HABITAT & BEHAVIOR: Tend to inhabit open areas of shallow to mid-range reefs where water flow is very strong. Most common between 30-70 feet. Polyps may be partially extended during the day.

NOTE: Also commonly known as Grooved Fungus Coral.

Rough Cactus Coral

Commonly the sharply protruding polyp mouths in the narrow valleys are pale and tinted in shades ranging from pink to red to orange.

ROUGH CACTUS CORAL
Mycetophyllia ferox

ORDER:
Scleractinia
FAMILY:
Mussidae
SUBFAMILY:
Mussinae

SIZE: Colony 1 - 2 ft.
DEPTH: 2 - 120 ft.

Rough Cactus Coral

Small colony with pale orange polyp mouths.

Rough Cactus Coral

Colony encrusting reef top.

Ridges may crisscross forming closed valleys and giving the colony a lattice-like appearance. Note the polyp mouths have a reddish tint.[far left]

Green variation. [left]

Fleshy Corals

VISUAL ID: Colonies thinly encrust, usually as circular plates, that generally conform to the contours of the substrate. Only member of the genus without central ridges. Surface covered with smooth, rounded bumps (polyp mouths). (Similar appearing deep colonies of Great Star Coral, *Montastraea cavernosa*, [pg. 127] are distinguished by well-defined corallites.) Shades of marbled green, brown, gray, blue-gray and may have iridescent tints. Colonies do not have tentacles.

ABUNDANCE & DISTRIBUTION: Occasional Bahamas, Caribbean. Not reported Florida.

HABITAT & BEHAVIOR: Inhabit shaded areas of deep reefs; most common along walls.

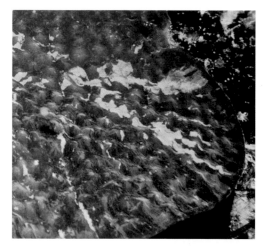

Ridgeless Cactus Coral
Color variation.

RIDGELESS CACTUS CORAL
Mycetophyllia reesi

ORDER:
Scleractinia
FAMILY:
Mussidae
SUBFAMILY:
Mussinae

SIZE: Colony 1 - 2 ft.
DEPTH: 60 - 220 ft.

Ridgeless Cactus Coral

Two colonies display blue and green color variations.

Note the smoothly rounded bumps that hold the polyp mouths at the top. [far left]

Occasionally pale patches highlight the polyp mouths. [left]

Ridgeless Cactus Coral

Color variation.

Fleshy Corals

VISUAL ID: Colonies form small, oval to hemispherical domes. Highly convoluted with fleshy ridges and deep, narrow valleys. (Small colonies of similar Ridged Cactus Coral, *Mycetophyllia lamarckiana*, [pg. 167] distinguished by wider valleys and less prominent ridges.) Colors quite variable, including shades of yellow, green, brown and gray. Occasionally iridescent tints of orange or blue. Ridges and valleys usually of contrasting shades or colors. Light colored, thin line along ridge tops.

ABUNDANCE & DISTRIBUTION: Populations highly variable from locality to locality; abundant to rare South Florida, Bahamas, Caribbean.

HABITAT & BEHAVIOR: Inhabit a wide range of shallow water environments, including fringing reefs, back reefs, patch reefs and areas with heavy sedimentation. Most common between 3-30 feet. Polyps retracted during day.

NOTE: Common name comes from sharp skeletal spines hidden under the fleshy tissue. Also commonly known as Cactus Coral, Fleshy Cactus Coral, and Stalked Cactus Coral.

VISUAL ID: Colonies form small oval to hemispherical domes. Fleshy ridges with rough, irregular closed polygonal valleys. Valleys usually contain only one or two polyps. Usually light or dark colored thin line along ridge tops. Ridges commonly brown or gray, occasionally green, pinkish or even purple; valleys commonly white or pale contrasting with darker ridges, but uncommonly dark matching ridges' color.

ABUNDANCE & DISTRIBUTION: Common to occasional South Florida, Bahamas, Caribbean.

HABITAT & BEHAVIOR: Inhabit a wide range of shallow water environments, including fringing, back, and patch reefs, and areas with heavy sedimentation. Most common between 10-35 feet. Polyps retracted during day.

NOTE: Formerly classified in genus *Isophyllastrea*. Also commonly known as Polygonal Coral.

SINUOUS CACTUS CORAL
Isophyllia sinuosa

ORDER:
Scleractinia
FAMILY:
Mussidae
SUBFAMILY:
Mussinae

SIZE: Colony 2 ½ - 8 in.
DEPTH: 3 - 85 ft.

ROUGH STAR CORAL
Isophyllia rigida

ORDER:
Scleractinia
FAMILY:
Mussidae
SUBFAMILY:
Mussinae

SIZE: Colony 3 - 7 in.
DEPTH: 3 - 65 ft.

Cup & Flower Corals

VISUAL ID: Single large, fleshy, circular to oval polyp. Underlying skeleton often evident in the form of raised radiating lines. Central area of corallite usually flat to slightly convex, rarely concave. Darker shades of gray to brown, green, and blue-green; base color often radially streaked with lighter shade. May fluoresce. Positive identification of this and the next two species requires magnified examination (see next description). There are no visual clues distinguishing Solitary Disk Coral, *Scolymia wellsi,* [next]. The Atlantic Mushroom, *S. lacera,* [next page] usually has a rougher texture and lighter colors.

ABUNDANCE & DISTRIBUTION: Occasional South Florida, Bahamas, Caribbean.

HABITAT & BEHAVIOR: Generally inhabit deep reefs and walls, occasionally shallower. Prefer shaded areas on rocky substrates and also grow in low-light conditions under ledge overhangs and in cave openings. Polyp tentacles retracted during day.

NOTE: Visual identification of pictured specimens was verified by collection and magnified examination of septa. Also commonly known as Smooth Disk Coral.

(USNM 91665) (USNM 91661)

VISUAL ID: Single large, fleshy, circular to oval polyp. Underlying skeleton often evident in the form of raised radiating lines. Central area of corallite usually flat to slightly concave, rarely convex. Darker shades of gray to brown, green, and blue-green; base color often radially streaked with lighter shade. May fluoresce. Smallest of the three disk coral species. Positive identification requires magnified examination of erect projections growing from the septa, known as teeth. This species has rough, irregular, thin, cylindrical teeth; Artichoke Coral, *Scolymia cubensis,* [previous] has spiky or pick-shaped teeth; and Atlantic Mushroom Coral, *S. lacera,* [next] has large triangular teeth.

ABUNDANCE & DISTRIBUTION: Occasional South Florida, Bahamas, Caribbean.

HABITAT & BEHAVIOR: Generally inhabit deep reefs and walls, occasionally shallower. Prefer shaded areas on rocky substrates and also grow in low-light conditions under ledge overhangs and in cave openings. Polyp tentacles retracted during day.

NOTE: Visual identification of pictured specimens was verified by collection and magnified examination of septa. (USMN 91560)

ARTICHOKE CORAL
Scolymia cubensis

ORDER:
Scleractinia
FAMILY:
Mussidae
SUBFAMILY:
Mussinae

SIZE: Polyp 1 ½ - 4 in.
DEPTH: 30 - 260 ft.

(USNM 91664)

SOLITARY DISK CORAL
Scolymia wellsi

ORDER:
Scleractinia
FAMILY:
Mussidae
SUBFAMILY:
Mussinae

SIZE: Polyp 1 - 2 ¾ in.
DEPTH: 30 - 260 ft.

Cup & Flower Corals

VISUAL ID: Single large, fleshy, circular to oval polyp with rough, warty texture. Central area of corallite usually concave to flat, rarely convex. Lighter shades of gray to green, blue-green and brown. (Generally texture rougher and color shades lighter than two previous species.) Caribbean's largest solitary polyp coral. Size alone can confirm identification if over four inches. If less, positive identification requires magnified examination of corallite structure (see previous description).

ABUNDANCE & DISTRIBUTION: Occasional South Florida, Bahamas, Caribbean.

HABITAT & BEHAVIOR: Inhabit deep reef environments and walls. Most common between 60-100 feet. Prefer well-lighted areas on rocky substrates and outcroppings. Polyp tentacles normally retracted during day, but may be extended in turbid conditions.

NOTE: Visual identification of pictured specimens was verified by magnified examination of triangular septal teeth.

VISUAL ID: Colonies formed of large fleshy polyps with rough, blemished texture. Although the polyps are well separated on the tips of a branched structure, their expanded fleshy tissues press against adjacent individuals so tightly that an overall colony appears as a solid mound. The polyp's skeleton, composed of numerous sharp spiky plates (septa) [above right], is the source of the common name. Shades of gray, may have tints of green, blue and even fluorescent reddish orange or pink (fluorescent color disappears if hand light or strobe are used).

ABUNDANCE & DISTRIBUTION: Common to occasional South Florida, Bahamas, Caribbean.

HABITAT & BEHAVIOR: Inhabit most reef environments; tolerate turbid environments. Most common between 20-80 feet. Polyps extend tentacles at night.

NOTE: Also commonly known as Large Flower Coral.

ATLANTIC MUSHROOM CORAL
Scolymia lacera

ORDER:
Scleractinia
FAMILY:
Mussidae
SUBFAMILY:
Mussinae

SIZE: Polyp 2½ - 6 in.
DEPTH: 30 - 260 ft.

SPINY FLOWER CORAL
Mussa angulosa

ORDER:
Scleractinia
FAMILY:
Mussidae
SUBFAMILY:
Mussinae

SIZE: Colony ½ - 2 ft.
Polyp 1½ - 4 in.
DEPTH: 5 - 180 ft.

Cup & Flower Corals

VISUAL ID: Clumps of widely spaced polyps on long stalks, that appear to originate from a central core, form hemispherical mounds. Corallites round to oval. Shades of yellow-brown to brown and gray, often with blue to blue-green to green tinting that may be somewhat iridescent. A rare variant, form *flabellata*, is distinguished by extremely long (up to six inches), narrow (about one-half inch) corallites.

ABUNDANCE & DISTRIBUTION: Common to occasional Florida, Bahamas, Caribbean; also north to North Carolina.

HABITAT & BEHAVIOR: Inhabit most reef environments, but prefer somewhat shaded, protected areas. Most common between 15-90 feet. Occasionally multiple colonies cover large area of the reef. Extend long translucent tentacles at night.

Smooth Flower Coral
Extended polyp detail.

Smooth Flower Coral
Corallite detail, typical form.

SMOOTH FLOWER CORAL
Eusmilia fastigiata
ORDER:
Scleractinia
FAMILY:
Meandrinidae

SIZE: Colony $1/2$ - $2\,1/2$ ft.
Corallite diameter $3/4$ - $1\,1/4$ in.
DEPTH: 3 - 200 ft.

Smooth Flower Coral
Colony with polyps extended at night.

Smooth Flower Coral
Corallite detail of Elongate Smooth Flower Coral, form flabellata.

Cup & Flower Corals

VISUAL ID: Brilliant red to orange or yellow polyp clumps that often form hemispherical mounds. Tissue covering skeleton usually deeper red to orange, while tentacles often bright orange to yellow. Colonies may contain only a few or hundreds of polyps. Ahermatypic and azooxanthellate.

ABUNDANCE & DISTRIBUTION: Scattered distribution throughout Florida, Bahamas, Caribbean. May be abundant in localized areas, but absent from similar environments around same island. A species native to the Indo-Pacific.

HABITAT & BEHAVIOR: Prefer shaded areas in a wide range of environments, including dock pilings, caves on shallow reefs, and undercuts on walls of deeper reefs. A clear water species that prefers some water movement. A few polyps may be extended during day, but full extension of entire colony normally occurs only at night.

NOTE: Orange Cup Coral is believed to be the only species of stony coral introduced to the western Atlantic. The species was first recorded in 1943 from Puerto Rico and Curacao. Interestingly some specimens collected in the Netherlands Antilles between 1948 and 1950 came from a ship's hull. Since that period the species abundance at these localities has been increasing. Orange Cup Coral has also been observed at numerous additional sites. If sighting dates and locations are plotted on a map it is easy to theorize that the species was transported into the Caribbean on a ship's bottom from either the eastern Pacific or tropical Indo-Pacific, where the opportunistic species is common, and has dispersed by following typical current patterns throughout the region. (Stephen D. Cairns, *Revision of the Shallow-Water Azooxanthellate Scleractinia of the Western Atlantic, Studies of the Natural History of the Caribbean Region*, 2000, Vol. 75)

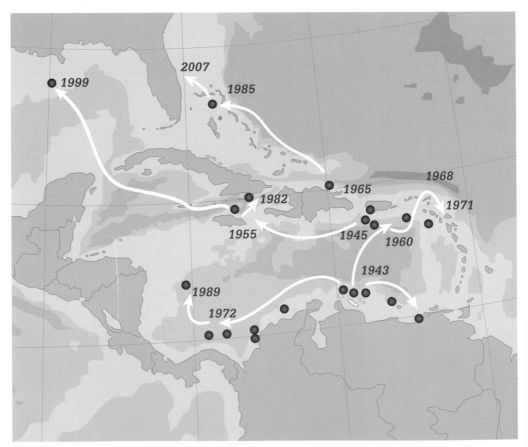

ORANGE CUP CORAL
Tubastraea coccinea

ORDER:
Scleractinia
FAMILY:
Dendrophylliidae

SIZE: Colony 3 - 12 in.
Corrallite diameter $1/2$ - $3/4$ in.
DEPTH: 3 - 120 ft.

Orange Cup Coral

Hemispherical colony.

*Colonies on
undercut reef face.*
[below left]

*Colonies on
dock piling at night.*
[below right]

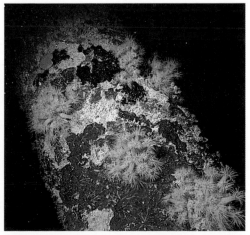

Cup & Flower Corals

VISUAL ID: Colonies and corallites are typically dark green, but can be medium green to nearly black. Tend to form bushy colonies with numerous tightly clustered and occasionally branching corallites. (Colonies in the species' native range of the Indo-West Pacific form large bushy branching structures. Scientists believe the Gulf of Mexico's (where the invasive species has been sighted) strong currents and frequent storms prevent taller stalks from forming.) Tufts of tentacles occasionally extend from the corallite cup during the day, but are open more commonly during periods of low light and especially at night. Ahermatypic and azooxanthellate.

ABUNDANCE & DISTRIBUTION: Rare Gulf of Mexico.

HABITAT & BEHAVIOR: An invasive species from the Indo-West Pacific that was first reported in 2006 on an oil rig platform near the entrance to New Orleans. It has spread at the time of this writing (2013) to at least nine additional platforms. It is known to be a prolific and may spread across the Tropical Western Atlantic much like its close relative Orange Cup Coral, *Tubastraea coccinea*, [previous page]. Sightings of the species should be reported to the Reef Environmental Education Foundation (REEF) at www.REEF.org, go to Programs – Exotic Species Sightings Program.

Baroque Cave Coral

Close-up of corallites growing from cave ceiling.

VISUAL ID: Colonial polyps often form small clusters. Corallites cone-shaped with circular to elliptical rims and deep central pits. Tall thin, rounded, protruding septa radiate from the pit and extend around the rim's lip. Often lavender or white, occasionally pink or pale green. Fragile. Ahermatypic and azooxanthellate.

ABUNDANCE & DISTRIBUTION: Occasional Caribbean. Not reported Florida or Bahamas.

HABITAT & BEHAVIOR: Inhabit the ceilings of caves, under ledge overhangs, usually with some water circulation. Most common below 80 feet.

NOTE: Visual identification of pictured specimens confirmed by collection (USNM 92084) and magnified examination.

GREEN CUP CORAL
Tubastraea micranthus

ORDER:
Scleractinia
FAMILY:
Dendrophylliidae

SIZE: $1/2$ - $1 1/2$ ft.
Corallite diameter $1/2$ in.
DEPTH: 3 - 150 ft.

Green Cup Coral

Colonies in the Gulf of Mexico oil rig platforms often mix with colonies of Orange Cup Coral [previous page].

BAROQUE CAVE CORAL
Thalamophyllia riisei

ORDER:
Scleractinia
FAMILY:
Caryophylliidae

SIZE: Corallite diameter
$1/4$ - $1/2$ in.
DEPTH: 50 - 1000 ft.

Cup & Flower Corals

VISUAL ID: Small solitary polyp. Corallite cone-shaped with base re-expanding to encrust and attach to hard substrate (occasionally free when base attaches to and envelopes a small pebble). Rim (calice) of corallite oval to elliptical. Twelve large septa of equal size with smaller septa between can be seen with an unaided eye. Small septal ridges continue down sides of corallite resulting in a corrugated texture. Red to pink, orange, light brown and white. Ahermatypic and azooxanthellate.

ABUNDANCE & DISTRIBUTION: Uncommon (within safe diving limits) Florida, Bahamas, Caribbean.

HABITAT & BEHAVIOR: Inhabit areas with hard substrates or gravel. Bases may be covered with sand or gravel exposing only the rims of corallites. Tend to inhabit shallower waters off Florida's northern coasts.

NOTE: Pictured specimen collected (USNM 92271) at 80 feet, off Jacksonville, Florida; identification confirmed by magnified examination.

VISUAL ID: Colonial; corallites may be clustered in small groups or appear to be solitary. Solitary examples are joined to nearby corallites by encrusting bases that may be hidden from view by overgrowing organisms. Corallites are slightly tapering and cylindrical with flared rims (calices). Six, tall, thick primary septa, and six smaller secondary septa can be seen by unaided eye. Fine septal ridges continue down sides of corallites resulting in a subtle corrugated texture, although not always obvious to the unaided eye. Bright orange to pink. Ahermatypic and azooxanthellate.

ABUNDANCE & DISTRIBUTION: Occasional Bahamas, Caribbean; also Gulf of Mexico.

HABITAT & BEHAVIOR: Inhabit dark recesses such as cave ceilings and under ledge overhangs.

NOTE: Identification of pictured specimens confirmed by collection and magnified examination: right (USNM 91651) at 15 feet, Roatan, Honduras; below (USNM 91655) at 65 ft, Conception Island, Bahamas; below right (USNM 91659) at 85 feet, San Salvador, Bahamas.

Orange Solitary Coral
Note corrugated texture on corallites' sides.

POROUS CUP CORAL
Balanophyllia floridana
ORDER:
Scleractinia
FAMILY:
Dendrophylliidae

SIZE: Corallite diameter
$^1/_2$ - 1 in.
DEPTH: 80 - 600 ft.

ORANGE SOLITARY CORAL
Rhizopsammia goesi
ORDER:
Scleractinia
FAMILY:
Dendrophylliidae

SIZE: Corallite diameter
$^1/_4$ - $^1/_2$ in.
DEPTH: 15 - 385 ft.

Orange Solitary Coral
*Solitary appearing
corallites are joined
by encrusting
bases.*

Cup & Flower Corals

VISUAL ID: Colonies form a thin encrusting base from which corallites protrude. Often the corallites appear unconnected because of overgrowing sponge, algae and other organisms, but the connection between two or three individuals is usually obvious. Corallites are circular to elliptical with tall, thin, rounded, protruding septa around the rims and deep central pits. There are usually twelve obvious, large septa of nearly equal size, and numerous smaller ones depending on corallite size. (Similar Lesser Speckled Cup Coral, *Colangia immersa*, [next] has only six large septa.) Orange-brown, brown, pink and lavender; central pit often pale green. Brown speckled pigmentation on septa is usual for this species. Occasionally large individual polyps do not show this pigmentation. Ahermatypic and azooxanthellate.

ABUNDANCE & DISTRIBUTION: Common Caribbean; occasional Florida, Bahamas.

HABITAT & BEHAVIOR: Inhabit the ceilings of caves, ledge overhangs, and occasionally on the ventral surface of deep sheet and plate corals.

(USNM 91652)   (USNM 92081)

VISUAL ID: Colonies form small encrusting groups of polyps. Often the corallites appear unconnected because of overgrowing sponge, algae and other organisms. Corallites are circular to elliptical with deep central pits. Six tall, thin, rounded septa protrude noticeably around the rim. (Similar Speckled Cup Coral, *Rhizosmilia maculata*, [previous] distinguished by twelve large septa of nearly equal size.) Numerous smaller septa are usually apparent. Light green, orange-brown, brown, pink, lavender and white. May have some brown speckled pigmentation. Center (mouth area of polyp) often of lighter and/or different color. Ahermatypic and azooxanthellate.

ABUNDANCE & DISTRIBUTION: Occasional Florida, Bahamas, Caribbean.

HABITAT & BEHAVIOR: Attach to and encrust the underside of plate corals, rocks, ledge overhangs and cave ceilings. Often only the top of the polyp is visible because the body is hidden by encrusting sponge, algae or other growths.

NOTE: Pictured specimens collected (USNM 91658) and visual identification confirmed by magnified examination.

SPECKLED CUP CORAL
Rhizosmilia maculata

ORDER:
Scleractinia
FAMILY:
Caryophylliidae

SIZE: Corallite diameter
¹/₄ - 1 in.
DEPTH: 10 - 500 ft.

Speckled Cup Coral
*Brown variation
with green centers;
note dark brown
speckles.*

Large solitary polyps.
[left]

LESSER SPECKLED CUP CORAL
Colangia immersa

ORDER:
Scleractinia
FAMILY:
Caryophylliidae

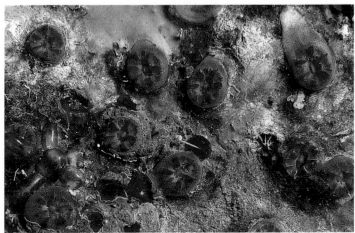

SIZE: Corallite diameter
¹/₄ - ³/₈ in.
DEPTH: 10 - 300 ft.

continued next page

Cup & Flower Corals

Lesser Speckled Cup Coral

Lavender variation encrusting underside of a ledge overhang.

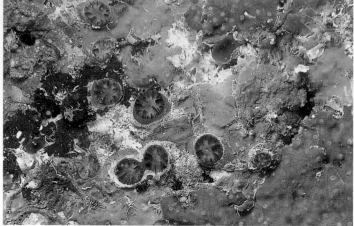

(USNM 92091)

VISUAL ID: Colonies form small encrusting groups of polyps. Often the corallites appear unconnected because of overgrowing sponge, algae and other organisms. Corallites are tall and cylindrical with sharp, prickly protrusions and deep central pits. Six tall, thin, rounded septa and six, somewhat smaller, secondary septa protrude noticeably around the circular rims. Smaller septa are usually apparent. White to brown with speckles. Ahermatypic and azooxanthellate.

ABUNDANCE & DISTRIBUTION: Rare Caribbean.

HABITAT & BEHAVIOR: Inhabit dark, deep recesses of cave ceilings. Other habitats unknown (see note). Often only the top of the polyp is visible because the body is hidden by encrusting sponge, algae or other growths.

NOTE: Pictured specimen collected (USMN 99247) at 35 feet, off Isla Cayos Cochinos, Honduras. Identification confirmed by magnified examination of corallites.

VISUAL ID: Colonies form small encrusting groups of polyps. Corallites circular with deep central pits. Six protruding primary and six, somewhat smaller, secondary septa around rims. Brown color, ranging from yellow-brown to brown to red-brown, is distinctive of this species. Never speckled like similar Speckled Cup Coral [previous page]. Ahermatypic and azooxanthellate.

ABUNDANCE & DISTRIBUTION: Occasional Florida, Bahamas, Caribbean.

HABITAT & BEHAVIOR: Attach to and encrust the underside of rocks, ledge overhangs and cave ceilings. Often only the top of the polyp is visible because the body is hidden by encrusting sponge, algae or other growths. Most common above 60 feet.

NOTE: There are two subspecies: *P. americana americana* from the western Atlantic; *P. americana mouchezii* from the eastern Atlantic.

Lesser Speckled Cup Coral

continued from previous page

Encrusting ceiling of a shallow tidal cave.

(USNM 92086)

CRYPTIC CAVE CORAL

Colangia jamaicaensis

ORDER:
Scleractinia
FAMILY:
Caryophylliidae

SIZE: Corallite diameter
$^1/_8$ - $^1/_4$ in.
DEPTH: 35 - 65 ft.

HIDDEN CUP CORAL

Phyllangia americana americana

ORDER:
Scleractinia
FAMILY:
Caryophylliidae

SIZE: Corallite diameter
$^1/_4$ - $^1/_2$ in.
DEPTH: 1 - 100 ft.

continued next page **191**

Cup & Flower Corals

Hidden Cup Coral

Colony on ceiling of shipwreck.

VISUAL ID: Colonies appear as scattered groups of tiny individual polyps; however, corallites in a colony are joined by a thin common base that is often obscured encrustations. Corallites cylindrical; septa often appear as rows of whitish dots radiating from centers and wrapping around rims. Shades of red-brown to brown. Ahermatypic and azooxanthellate.

ABUNDANCE & DISTRIBUTION: Occasional Florida, Bahamas, Caribbean.

HABITAT & BEHAVIOR: Attach to and encrust the underside of rocks, coral rubble, ledge overhangs and cave ceilings. Often only the tip of the polyp is visible because the body is hidden by encrusting sponge, algae or other growths. Most common above 20 feet.

NOTE: Visual identification of pictured specimens confirmed by collection (USNM 92090) and magnified examination.

Dwarf Cup Coral

Encrusting wall of cave.

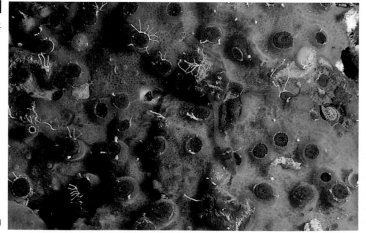

(USNM 91656)

Hidden Cup Coral
continued from previous page

Yellow-brown variation.

(USNM 92086)

DWARF CUP CORAL
Astrangia solitaria
ORDER:
Scleractinia
FAMILY:
Rhizangiidae

SIZE: Corallite diameter
$1/8$ - $1/4$ in.
DEPTH: 1 - 135 ft.

Dwarf Cup Coral
Polyps extended.

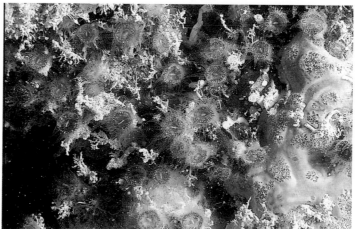

(USNM 91657)

Cup & Flower Corals

VISUAL ID: Colonies form clusters of circular to oval corallites with common encrusting base. Numerous tall rounded septa and separated inner ends of septa (pali) inside central pit visible to unaided eye. Colonies expand by asexual budding from the edges of common base. Septa red-brown; pali and central pit white. Ahermatypic and azooxanthellate.

ABUNDANCE & DISTRIBUTION: Uncommon Bahamas, Caribbean; also Gulf of Mexico.

HABITAT & BEHAVIOR: Attach to and encrust the underside ledge overhangs and cave ceilings.

NOTE: Pictured specimen collected (USNM 92280) at 125 feet, off West Caicos, Turks & Caicos Islands and visual identification confirmed by magnified examination.

VISUAL ID: Colonies formed by circular corallites with common encrusting base. Six to twelve high rounded septa, with several smaller septa between and numerous lobes in central pit are visible to an unaided eye. Colonies expand by asexual budding from the edges of common base. Shades of white, occasionally tinted with pink. Ahermatypic and azooxanthellate.

ABUNDANCE & DISTRIBUTION: Rare off West Palm Beach, Florida. Additional distribution unknown (See note).

HABITAT & BEHAVIOR: Attach to and encrust the underside ledge overhangs and cave ceilings.

NOTE: Formerly an undescribed species discovered by Paul Humann at 70 feet off Palm Beach, FL. and named in his honor. (USNM 92080)

VISUAL ID: Solitary circular to slightly elliptical corallites with twelve large rounded septa with three smaller septa between pairs of larger septa are visible to an unaided eye. Separated inner ends of septa (pali) form a light colored elliptical ring around deep central pit. Upper half of corallite shades of brown; basal deposits creamy white. Ahermatypic and azooxanthellate.

ABUNDANCE & DISTRIBUTION: Uncommon Bahamas, Caribbean. Not reported Florida.

HABITAT & BEHAVIOR: Firmly attach to hard substrate on the underside of ledge overhangs and cave ceilings. Occasionally in the recesses of small cavities.

NOTE: Pictured specimen collected (USNM 91667) at 70 feet, off San Salvador, Bahamas; visual identification confirmed by magnified examination.

TWOTONE CUP CORAL
Phacelocyathus flos
ORDER:
Scleractinia
FAMILY:
Caryophylliidae

SIZE: Corallite diameter
$^1/_4$ - $^1/_2$ in.
DEPTH: 70 - 1700 ft.

ORNATE CUP CORAL
Coenocyathus humanni
ORDER:
Scleractinia
FAMILY:
Caryophylliidae

SIZE: Corallite diameter
$^1/_8$ - $^1/_4$ in.
DEPTH: 70 ft. (see note)

BUTTON CUP CORAL
Coenocyathus caribbeana
ORDER:
Scleractinia
FAMILY:
Caryophylliidae

SIZE: Corallite diameter
$^1/_8$ - $^1/_4$ in.
DEPTH: 50 - 550 ft.

Class Anthozoa
Order Antipatharia

(An-tih-path-AIR-ee-ah / Gr. against disease)

Black Corals

Black corals are generally thought to be deep dwellers, but about half of the approximately 30 species in the Caribbean area can be found within safe scuba diving depths and several grow in surprisingly shallow water. Black coral polyps secrete a protein material, usually black in color, that becomes extremely hard and strong by a tanning process. This material is laid down in **concentric layers** forming branched or wire-like structures (skeleton). When a branch is crosscut these layers resemble the growth rings of a tree. The branching pattern of many species is unique and often the key to visual identification. Several species have tiny branchlets called **pinnules.**

Black coral polyps do not form corallite "homes" like stony corals, but instead simply live on the skeletal surface. Each polyp has six small, non-retractable **tentacles** that can, however, expand or contract to some degree. The tentacles are normally visible to the unaided eye and are an important key in recognizing a colonial structure as black coral. The individual polyps of many species are recognizable because they are spaced apart from one another and their clusters of tentacles resemble barbs of barbed wire. Polyps of other species are spaced close so together that they are difficult to distinguish and appear as a mass of inseparable tentacles.

The polyp tissue of most black corals is somewhat translucent and color pigments only tint the colony gray, brown, rust-red, or green. Occasionally the pigments may be intense and dramatic, especially wire corals which are bright yellow-green or red.

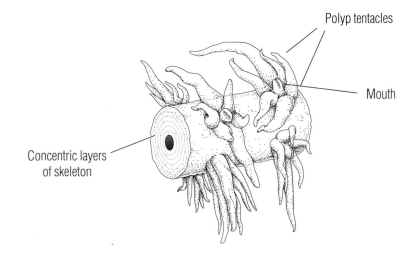

Polyp tentacles

Mouth

Concentric layers
of skeleton

A few black coral species attain considerable size and their branches are collected, cut, fashioned, polished and sold by jewelers as a semiprecious material. The value of these trinkets comes more from jewelers' propaganda of rareness and the danger associated with deep diving to collect branches, than from any innate property of the material itself. In fact, the black coral species most frequently used by jewelers is neither rare or found particularly deep — on occasion a snorkeler might even sight a colony! Unfortunately, it is now rare in many areas from over collecting. The great black coral forests of Grand Cayman and Cozumel are only a memory. It will take these slow growing colonies over 100 years to reestablish themselves.

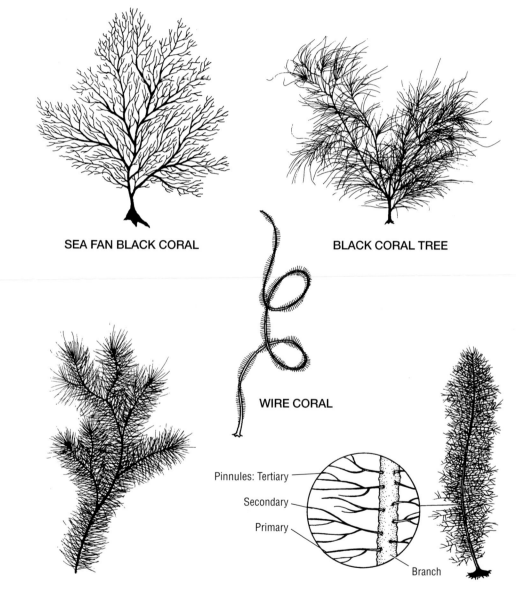

SEA FAN BLACK CORAL

BLACK CORAL TREE

WIRE CORAL

Pinnules: Tertiary
Secondary
Primary
Branch

BOTTLE-BRUSH BUSH BLACK CORAL

BOTTLE BRUSH BLACK CORAL

Black Corals

VISUAL ID: Bushy branched colonies of primary stalks, with long thin, scraggly branchlets. Primary branches golden-brown to brown to black and may be tinted red, green or blue. Branchlets are often of lighter color. It is now rare to see colonies over four feet in height because of over collecting (see note).

ABUNDANCE & DISTRIBUTION: Common to uncommon Bahamas, Caribbean; rare South Florida. Because of over collecting, now rare in many locations.

HABITAT & BEHAVIOR: In shallow water, occasionally inhabit caves and under large overhangs. In deep water, primarily inhabit canyons and wall faces with some current or periodic water movement. Most common between 80 and 240 feet; in many locations rarely found above 150 feet because of over collecting.

NOTE: This species, prized by the jewelry industry, is often called Kings Coral.

SIMILAR SPECIES: *Antipathes salix,* often confused with this species, is common between 300-1000 feet.

(USNM 92276)

VISUAL ID: Profuse primary and secondary branches extend from a holdfast in nearly a single plane. Thin pinnate branchlets line either side of the secondary branches, resembling large feathers. Primary and secondary branches golden-brown to brown, gray, or black; may be tinted red, green or blue. Branchlets are often of lighter color.

ABUNDANCE & DISTRIBUTION: Common to uncommon Bahamas, Caribbean; rare South Florida.

HABITAT & BEHAVIOR: In shallow water, inhabit caves and under large overhangs. In deep water, inhabit most reef environments including reef slopes, and along walls. Most common between 60 and 180 feet. Often grow inside old deep shipwrecks. A few species of small stalked barnacles and other invertebrates regularly live in association this coral.

NOTE: Formerly classified in the genus *Antipathes*.

BUSHY BLACK CORAL
Antipathes caribbeana
ORDER:
Antipatharia
Family:
Antipathidae

Bushy colony.
[far left]

Branch/polyp detail.
[left]

SIZE: 2 - 12 ft.
DEPTH: 40 - 300 ft.

**FEATHER
BLACK CORAL**
Plumapathes pennacea
ORDER:
Antipatharia
Family:
Myriopathidae

SIZE: 1 - 5 ft.
DEPTH: 15 - 1000 ft.

continued next page

Black Corals

VISUAL ID: Upright colonies of stiff coarse, primary and secondary branches extend in nearly a single plane. Occasionally somewhat bushy. Bright orangish brown to orange-red. (Similar Gray Sea Fan Black Coral, *Antipathes atlantica*, [next] distinguished by gray to greenish color, with network of fine, delicate branches.)

ABUNDANCE & DISTRIBUTION: Occasional Bahamas, Caribbean; rare South Florida.

HABITAT & BEHAVIOR: Inhabit most deep environments, often at the base of walls or in the open on reef tops. Prefer areas with good water circulation. Generally inhabit more open areas than similar Gray Sea Fan Black Coral.

Orange Sea Fan Black Coral

Sparsely branched colony.

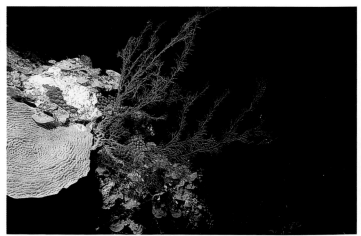

Feather
Black Coral
continued from
previous page

Branchlet/polyp detail

Grayish variation.
[far left]

Golden brown variation.
[left]

ORANGE SEA FAN
BLACK CORAL
Antipathes gracilis
ORDER:
Antipathidae
Family:
Myriopathidae

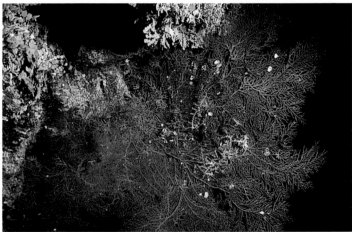

SIZE: 1¹/₂ - 4 ft.
DEPTH: 60 - 300 ft.

Orange Sea Fan
Black Coral
Unusual thickly
branched colony.

Black Corals

VISUAL ID: Colonies shaped like large classic sea fans with radiating primary branches and a network of numerous, fine, delicate, occasionally interconnecting secondary branches. Polyps shades of pale gray, sometimes tinged with pink, to greenish gray and dark gray; branches black. (Similar Orange Sea Fan Black Coral, *Cupressopathes gracilis,* [previous] distinguished by bright orangish brown to red-brown color, and heavier, coarser, more bushy branches.)

ABUNDANCE & DISTRIBUTION: Occasional Bahamas, Caribbean; rare South Florida.

HABITAT & BEHAVIOR: Inhabit shaded deep reef environments, especially in canyons, crevices, under ledge overhangs and along walls where there is good water circulation. Generally more reclusive than similar Orange Sea Fan Black Coral.

Gray Sea Fan Black Coral
Unusually bushy colony.

VISUAL ID: Colonies form highly, subdivided tangled networks of fine branches that contour to the substrate. (Similar Scraggly Black Coral, *Antipathes umbratica,* [next] distinguished by thicker, rigid, coarse branches.) Colonies do not protrude more than an inch or so above the substrate. Shades of brown to gray.

ABUNDANCE & DISTRIBUTION: Common Bahamas, Caribbean; occasional to uncommon South Florida.

HABITAT & BEHAVIOR: Inhabit shaded areas under ledge overhangs, cave ceilings and recessed wall faces.

NOTE: Pictured specimen collected (USNM 92277) at 90 feet, off Roatan, Honduras; visual identification confirmed by laboratory examination.

GRAY SEA FAN BLACK CORAL
Antipathes atlantica

ORDER:
Antipatharia
Family:
Antipathidae

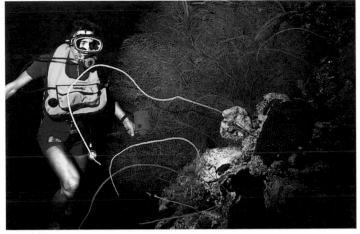

SIZE: 1^1/$_2$ - 4 ft.
DEPTH: 60 - 300 ft.

Gray Sea Fan Black Coral
Note delicate net-like structure.

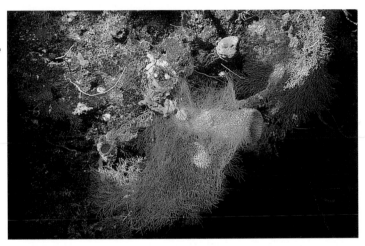

HAIR NET BLACK CORAL
Antipathes lenta

ORDER:
Antipatharia
Family:
Antipathidae

SIZE: 4 - 10 in.
DEPTH: 80 - 250 ft.

VISUAL ID: Colonies, with a single holdfast, form bush-like tangles of rigid, coarse branches that contour to the substrate. (Similar Hair Net Black Coral, *Antipathes lenta,* [previous] distinguished by finer, more flexible branches.) Colonies do not protrude more than an inch or so above the substrate. Stalk structures gray to black; expanded polyp tentacles pale to translucent.

ABUNDANCE & DISTRIBUTION: Common Bahamas. Caribbean.

HABITAT & BEHAVIOR: Inhabit shaded areas under ledge overhangs, cave ceilings and undercut wall faces.

NOTE: Pictured specimen collected (USNM 92274) at 90 feet, off Roatan, Honduras; visual identification confirmed by laboratory examination.

VISUAL ID: Bushy upright colonies formed by openly branched primary and secondary stalks. (Similar Scraggly Bottle-brush Black Coral, *Tanacetipathes barbadensis,* [next] is more sparsely branched.) Numerous pinnules extend radially from stalks. Primary pinnules both long and short. There are occasional secondary pinnules, but tertiary pinnules are rare. Shades of gray to greenish gray and olive. Young colonies may have only a single unbranched stalk and require microscopic examination for positive identification.

ABUNDANCE & DISTRIBUTION: Occasional to uncommon Florida, Bahamas, Caribbean.

HABITAT & BEHAVIOR: Inhabit deep reefs and gently sloping drop-offs.

NOTE: Formerly classified in the genus *Antipathes*.

VISUAL ID: Colonies formed by sparsely branched primary and secondary stalks. (Similar Bottle-brush Bush Black Coral, *Tanacetipathes hirta,* [previous] is more heavily branched.) Numerous pinnules extend radially from stalks. Primary pinnules long and generally of equal length. There are occasional secondary pinnules, but tertiary pinnules are rare. Shades of gray. Young colonies may have only single, unbranched stalks.

ABUNDANCE & DISTRIBUTION: Occasional to uncommon Florida, Bahamas, Caribbean.

HABITAT & BEHAVIOR: Inhabit deep reefs and gently sloping drop-offs; occasionally in old shipwrecks.

NOTE: Pictured colony is young and just starting to branch near base. Positive identification requires microscopic examination. Pictured specimen collected (USNM 92278) at 90 feet, off West Palm Beach, Florida; visual identification confirmed in laboratory. Formerly classified in the genus *Antipathes*.

204

SCRAGGLY
BLACK CORAL
Antipathes umbratica
ORDER:
Antipatharia
Family:
Antipathidae

SIZE: 6 - 12 in.
DEPTH: 60 - 250 ft.

BOTTLE-BRUSH BUSH
BLACK CORAL
Tanacetipathes hirta
ORDER:
Antipatharia
Family:
Myriopathidae

SIZE: 1 - 2¹/₂ ft.
Pinnules 1 - 2 in.
DEPTH: 90 - 200 ft.

SCRAGGLY
BOTTLE-BRUSH
BLACK CORAL
*Tanacetipathes
barbadensis*
ORDER:
Antipatharia
Family:
Myriopathidae

SIZE: 1 - 2 ft.
Pinnules 2 in.
DEPTH: 90 - 200 ft.

VISUAL ID: Colonies formed by long, unbranched primary stalks from which numerous pinnules extend radially. Both secondary and tertiary pinnules common, giving the stalks a bushier appearance than Bottle-brush Bush Black Coral, *Tanacetipathes hirta,* [previous page middle] or Scraggly Bottle-brush Black Coral, *T. barbadensis,* [previous]. Colonies may be solitary, but often grow in clusters. Shades of gray.

ABUNDANCE & DISTRIBUTION: Occasional to uncommon Florida, Bahamas, Caribbean.

HABITAT & BEHAVIOR: Inhabit deep reefs and drop-offs; occasionally in old shipwrecks.

NOTE: Positive identification requires microscopic examination. Pictured specimen collected (USNM 92279) at 90 feet, off West Palm Beach, Florida; visual identification confirmed in laboratory. Formerly classified in the genus *Antipathes.*

VISUAL ID: Colonies form long single, unbranched, wire-like stalks that often twist and coil. May appear fuzzy, the result of polyp tentacles extending from stalk surface. Shades of yellow, yellow-brown, red-brown, brown and green. Without artificial light some colonies appear chartreuse.

ABUNDANCE & DISTRIBUTION: Common South Florida, Bahamas, Caribbean.

HABITAT & BEHAVIOR: Inhabit a wide range of deep water environments, but most common in narrow, deep-cut canyons and along vertical wall faces. May appear as the predominant life form on some deep walls. Most abundant at depths below 90 feet.

NOTE: Recent DNA studies show that *Cirrhipathes* and *Stichopathes* are separate genera and species *lutkeni* should be identified as *Stichopathes lutkeni.*

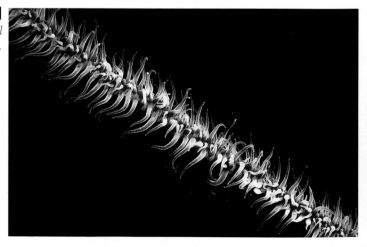

Wire Coral
Branch/polyp detail
of red variation.

BOTTLE-BRUSH BLACK CORAL

Tanacetipathes tanacetum

ORDER:
Antipatharia
Family:
Myriopathidae

SIZE: 4 - 10 in.
Pinnules ³/₄ - 1 ¹/₂ in.
DEPTH: 85 - 250 ft.

WIRE CORAL

Stichopathes luetkeni

ORDER:
Antipatharia
Family:
Antipathidae

SIZE: 1¹/₂ - 14 ft.
DEPTH: 45 - 375 ft.

APPENDIX I

Marine Plants & Algae

Kingdom Plantae
Kingdom Protista

Marine plants and algae (primarily phytoplankton) form the base of the oceanic food chain. All are photosynthetic, taking energy from sunlight and nutrients from the water or substrate, producing the food and oxygen used (either directly or indirectly) by other organisms to sustain life. Because they require sunlight for their vital processes, most grow intertidally to just over 100 feet. A few species grow deeper, and in the extremely clear water of the Caribbean some species may be found at surprising depths. There are over 600 species reported in the western tropical Atlantic. Those included in this text are the more common species growing on coral reefs and adjacent environments.

Marine plants, like their terrestrial counterparts, have true roots (containing conductive tissue), stems, leaves and flowers. Algae (singular alga) have no true roots, but attach to the substrate by holdfast structures called **rhizoids**, and runners connecting upright blades, called **rhizomes**. The upright parts of the plant are called **stalks** rather than stems, and **blades** instead of leaves. Several species of algae have bulb-like structures containing gas, called **bladders or floats,** that keep the structure upright. Most common marine algae can be visually identified by the shape of their blades and branching pattern. Algae are classified into Phyla on the basis of their predominate photosynthetic pigment. Although all contain some chlorophyll, only one group of algae is green.

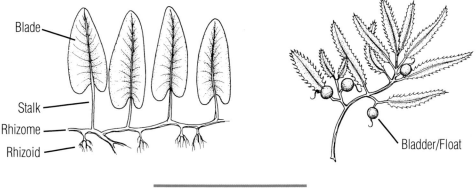

Flowering Plants

CLASS: Angiospermae (AN-gih-oo-sperm-uh/Gr. vessel and seed)

There are only a few species of marine flowering plants. Those most commonly observed by divers are the sea grasses (not related to terrestrial grasses) that often grow in great beds in areas of sand and sandy rubble adjacent to reefs. There are only three common species, and each can be easily distinguished by the size and shape of its leaves.

Brown Algae

PHYLUM: Phaeophyta (Fay-OH-fita/Gr. dusky plant)

The two best known algae are both brown: Kelp, which grows primarily in the temperate latitudes of western North and South America; and Sargassum of the tropical and subtropical latitudes of the western Atlantic. Gas filled floats keep Kelp upright and Sargassum floating on the surface. Brown algae ranges in color from shades of pale creamy brown to yellow-brown, green-brown and dark brown. Occasionally they are marked with shades of yellow, green and/or blue. Color is primarily the result of a brown pigment called fucoxanthin. Several species of brown algae are common inhabitants of the reef.

Green Algae

PHYLUM: Chlorophyta (Klor-OH-fita/Gr. green plant)

Generally the most commonly observed algae on tropical reefs are green. They are both abundant and represented by a large number of species. Many are calcareous and along with coralline red algae add significant amounts of calcium carbonate to the reefs, as well as, much of the brilliant white sand found on and around reefs. Green algae grow in a wide range of patterns, including single-celled bubble-like plants to fan-like blades, bristly brushes, hanging vines and serrated edged, upright blades. Chlorophyll is the pigment primarily responsible for their color, which ranges from shades of pale mint green to bright Kelly green, yellowish-green, brownish-green and dark green.

Red Algae

PHYLUM: Rhodophyta (Rode-OH-fita/Gr. rose-red plant)

Red algae, although abundant on tropical reefs, often goes unnoticed because of their generally dull coloration and nondescript growth forms. They are the most diversified of the algae, with over 4,000 tropical species. Calcareous species are important and integral elements in the reef building process. Many of those adding calcium carbonate to the reef are encrusting and appear as nothing more than a dull red to lavender to purple coloration of the rocky substrate. Reef crests exposed to vigorous wave activity are often thoroughly cemented by the activity of calcareous red algae, forming a reef zone called the algal ridge. Algal ridges can be found along the exposed reefs of the Windward Islands, Panama and St. Croix. Many non-coralline red algae are weed-like, growing in reddish translucent tangles, while others appear mossy or fuzzy. The primary red-pink pigment phycoerythrin, in combination with other pigments, is responsible for colors that range from pale pink to lavender, purple, brown-red and dark burgundy red.

Seagrasses & Brown Algae

TURTLE GRASS
Thalassia testudinum
Seagrasses – Angiospermae
SIZE: Height 4 - 24 in.
ID: Generally erect, ribbon-shaped green leaves with rounded tips. Have extensive root system with well anchored runners. Produce tiny pale pink to greenish white flowers. Leaves often covered with sediment and encrusting organisms. Grow on sandy bottoms and areas of mixed sand and coral rubble. Form extensive beds that can cover large areas. Often mix with Manatee Grass, *Syringodium filiforme*, beds [below]. Most common between 0-25 ft. Abundant Florida, Bahamas, Caribbean.

MANATEE GRASS *Syringodium filiforme*
SIZE: Height 2 - 18 in.   Seagrasses – Angiospermae
ID: Generally erect, thin, stem-like, cylindrical green leaves. Extensive network of runners. Often covered with sediment and encrusting organisms. Grow on sandy bottom often mixing with Turtle Grass [above]. Common Florida, Bahamas, Caribbean.

MIDRIB SEAGRASS *Halophila baillonis*
SIZE: Height 1 - 2 in.   Seagrasses – Angiospermae
ID: Generally erect, flat elongated-oval, green leaves with distinctive midribs; older leaves often rippled. Regularly covered with sediment and encrusting organisms. Inhabit muddy bottoms to sandy areas. Occasional Florida, Bahamas, Caribbean.

SARGASSUM SEAWEED
Sargassum fluitans
Brown Algae – Phaeophyta
SIZE: Blades 1 - 2 in.
ID: Individual plants join to form dense, relatively thick, floating mats that can cover huge areas of the surface. Often mix with Sargasso Weed, *S. natans*, [below]. Thin smooth-branching stalks bear long, serrated blades and spherical gas-filled floats that keep the plants afloat. Shades of brown; blades have a distinctive central vein of a lighter shade. Abundant to common South Florida, Bahamas, Caribbean.

SARGASSO WEED
Sargassum natans
Brown Algae – Phaeophyta
SIZE: Blades 1 - 2 in.
ID: Individual plants join to form dense floating mats that often cover huge areas of the surface. Typically mix with Sargassum Seaweed, *S. fluitans*, [above]. Thin spiny, branching stalks bear long thin, serrated blades without a prominent central vein. Spherical gas-filled floats tipped with small spines keep the plants afloat. Shades of brown. Abundant to common South Florida, Bahamas, Caribbean.

Brown Algae

SARGASSUM ALGAE
Sargassum spp.
Brown Algae – Phaeophyta
SIZE: Height 4 in. - 5 ft.
ID: Several species of *Sargassum* attach to the substrate and grow in bushy, upright forms. Long, oval-shaped blades may have smooth or striated edges. Blades and clusters of spherical gas-filled floats are attached to smooth, cylindrical stalks. Whitish brown to brown, brown-green and olive. Positive identification to species requires laboratory exam. Inhabit most environments. Common to occasional Florida, Bahamas, Caribbean.

WHITE-VEIN SARGASSUM
Sargassum hystrix
Brown Algae – Phaeophyta
SIZE: Height 4 - 16 in.
ID: Long, oval-shaped blades shades of brown to dark olive; distinctive white central veins. Blades attached to smooth, cylindrical stalks. Can be somewhat bushy. Grow in most environments, including reefs. Most common on deep patch reefs and adjacent areas. Common to occasional South Florida, Bahamas, Caribbean.

Y-BRANCHED ALGAE
Dictyota spp.
Brown Algae – Phaeophyta
SIZE: Height 4 - 18 in.
ID: There are several species in this genus that are difficult to distinguish visually. All have branches that fork near the ends. Tips may be round or pointed. Typically form mats of dense to loosely packed flat blades that overgrow substrate. Light to medium brown and/or green to blue-green, occasionally with bright blue tint. Can spread to cover large areas. Abundant South Florida, Bahamas, Caribbean.

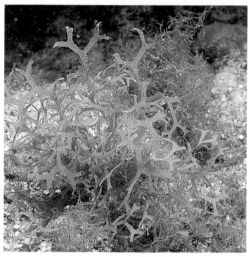

SERRATED STRAP ALGA
Dictyota ciliolata
Brown Algae – Phaeophyta
SIZE: Height 4 - 6 in.
ID: Bushy clumps of strap-like blades that have distinctive points along edges. Irregularly branched. Light yellow-brown to brown with light, wavy pattern; may have greenish tints. Grow in most reef habitats. Attach to rocky substrates, often in exposed areas with surge. Abundant South Florida, Bahamas, Caribbean.

Brown Algae

LEAFY FLAT-BLADE ALGA
Stypopodium zonale
Brown Algae – Phaeophyta
SIZE: 4 - 16 in.
ID: Bushy plant formed by flat, squared-off blades that are irregularly branched and split. Concentrically banded in a wide range of colors, including shades of yellow, yellow-green, green, brown-green, brown; often with tints of iridescent green and/or blue. Attach to rocky substrates. Often abundant in shallow water, less common on deeper reefs. Abundant to occasional South Florida, Bahamas, Caribbean.

LEAFY ROLLED-BLADE ALGA
Padina boergesenii
Brown Algae – Phaeophyta
SIZE: 4 - 6 in.
ID: Form large, dense clumps of leafy blades with rounded, often semicircular outer margins. Blades are irregularly split and branched. Concentrically banded in a wide range of colors from yellow to green, brown and blue. Attach to rocky substrates. Often abundant in shallow water, less common on deeper reefs. Abundant to occasional South Florida, Bahamas, Caribbean.

WHITE SCROLL ALGA
Padina sanctae-crucis
Brown Algae – Phaeophyta
SIZE: Blades 2 - 6 in.
ID: Form large dense clumps of leafy blades with rounded, semicircular outer margins. Blades are irregularly split and branched. Concentrically banded in shades of white to grayish white, tan and light yellowish brown. Attach to rocky substrates in most marine habitats, especially shallow reef flats. Abundant to occasional South Florida, Bahamas, Caribbean.

ENCRUSTING FAN-LEAF ALGA   *Lobophora variegata*
SIZE: Blades 1 - 6 in.   Brown Algae – Phaeophyta
ID: Thin fan blades encrust substrate, often overlapping in a shingle-like pattern. Shades of green to brown and tan. Encrust large areas of shaded, rocky substrates. Abundant to common South Florida, Bahamas, Caribbean.

SWISS CHEESE ALGA   *Hydroclathrus clathratus*
SIZE: 3 in. - 3 ft.   Brown Algae – Phaeophyta
ID: A spongy-looking mass of tangled interconnected branches with numerous irregular-sized holes. No permanent attachment; lay inside depressions. Shades of brown. Abundant to common Florida; occasional to rare Bahamas, Caribbean.

SAUCER LEAF ALGA   *Turbinaria tricostata*
SIZE: 4 - 16 in.   Brown Algae – Phaeophyta
ID: Erect central column with branches bearing clumps of triangular, cone-shaped blades with saucer-like tips. Shades of brown, often with dark brown speckles. Shallow lagoons and back reef areas. Occasional Florida, Bahamas, Caribbean.

BLISTERED SAUCER LEAF ALGA   *Turbinaria turbinata*
SIZE: 4 - 16 in.   Brown Algae – Phaeophyta
ID: Erect central column with branches bearing clumps of triangular, cone-shaped blades with saucer-like tips with a distinctive blister-like swelling at center. Shades of brown, often with dark speckles. Occasional Florida, Bahamas, Caribbean.

Green Algae

WATERCRESS ALGA
Halimeda opuntia
Green Algae – Chlorophyta
SIZE: Segments ¹/₈ - ³/₈ in.
ID: Thick, profusely branched clumps of rounded, three – lobed or ribbed, leaf-like segments. Spread laterally to cover large areas of reef or sand. Dark to bright green and yellowish green. Grow in shallow depressions, cracks and crevices between hard corals and other protected areas. Abundant South Florida, Bahamas, Caribbean.

LARGE LEAF WATERCRESS ALGA   *Halimeda discoidea*
SIZE: Segments ³/₈ - 1 ¹/₂ in.   Green Algae – Chlorophyta
ID: Branched clumps of smooth, fan- or disk-shaped segments. Attach by a short holdfast; tend to grow in a single plane. Shades of green. Largest segments in genus. Abundant to common South Florida, Bahamas, Caribbean.

STALKED LETTUCE LEAF ALGA   *Halimeda tuna*
SIZE: Segments ¹/₂ - ³/₄ in.   Green Algae – Chlorophyta
ID: Branched clumps of thin rounded, fan or disk-shaped segments. Attached by stalk formed of basal segments. Shades of green. Grow in most marine environments. Abundant to common South Florida, Bahamas, Caribbean.

SMALL-LEAF HANGING VINE *Halimeda goreaui*
SIZE: Segments ⅛ - ¼ in. Green Algae – Chlorophyta
ID: Long chains of rounded, three-lobed, small leaf-like segments. Chains are most commonly unbranched and often hang in shaded areas from ledge overhangs. Shades of green. Abundant to common South Florida, Bahamas, Caribbean.

LARGE-LEAF HANGING VINE *Halimeda copiosa*
SIZE: Segments ½ - ¾ in. Green Algae – Chlorophyta
ID: Long chains of rounded, rectangular, relatively large leaf-like segments. Chains frequently branch and often hang in shaded areas from ledge overhangs. Shades of green. Abundant to common South Florida, Bahamas, Caribbean.

BULBOUS LETTUCE LEAF ALGA *Halimeda lacrimosa*
SIZE: Segments ¼ in. Green Algae – Chlorophyta
ID: Chains of spherical or bulbous segments, resembling strings of beads, without distinct stalks. Green to pale green to whitish. Grow on reefs and rocky substrates. Common to occasional South Florida, Bahamas, Cuba. Not reported remainder of Caribbean.

THREE FINGER LEAF ALGA *Halimeda incrassata*
SIZE: Height 4 - 10 in. Green Algae – Chlorophyta
ID: Upright, occasionally branched, chains of distinctive three-lobed, leaf-like segments. Stiff primary stalk. Shades of green. Grow in shallow sandy areas, may mix with seagrass. Abundant to common South Florida, Bahamas, Caribbean.

Green Algae

GREEN JOINTED-STALK ALGA *Halimeda monile*
SIZE: Height 3 - 8 in. Green Algae – Chlorophyta
ID: Upright, occasionally branched, chains of cylindrical to somewhat flattened segments. Branch from three-lobed segments. Relatively stiff structure. Shades of green. Grow in sandy areas. Occasional South Florida, Bahamas, Caribbean.

FUZZY TIP ALGA *Neomeris annulata*
SIZE: Height 3/4 - 1 1/2 in. Green Algae – Chlorophyta
ID: Small, cylindrical, ringed stalks with fuzzy tips. May grow singly or in compact clumps. Tips green; stalks white with greenish tints. Grow in sand and rubble areas, often in shade. Occasional South Florida, Bahamas, Caribbean.

FLAT-TOP BRISTLE BRUSH *Penicillus pyriformis*
SIZE: Height 2 - 4 1/2 in. Green Algae – Chlorophyta
ID: Cone-shaped, tightly packed bristle-like filaments, with flattish top. Tip of cone merges into heavy, short stalk anchored in sand. Dark green to gray-green. Grow in sandy, protected areas. Occasional South Florida, Bahamas, Caribbean.

BRISTLE BALL BRUSH *Penicillus dumetosus*
SIZE: Height 2 - 6 in. Green Algae – Chlorophyta
ID: Spherical ball of tightly packed bristle-like filaments that merge into a heavy, short stalk anchored in sand. Dark green to gray-green. Grow in sandy, protected areas. Occasional South Florida, Bahamas, Caribbean.

GREEN FEATHER ALGA *Caulerpa sertularioides*
SIZE: Height 4 - 8 in. Green Algae – Chlorophyta
ID: Tall stiff, feather-like structures grow upward from long, cylindrical, attached runners. Pinnate branchlets are cylindrical with sharp points. Light green. Grown in shallow sandy areas. Occasional South Florida, Bahamas, Caribbean.

FLAT GREEN FEATHER ALGA *Caulerpa mexicana*
SIZE: Height 1 - 8 in. Green Algae – Chlorophyta
ID: Flat feather-like structures grow upward from long, cylindrical attached runners. Pinnate branchlets have sharp points and taper to the midrib. Yellow-green to green. Grow in sand. Occasional South Florida, Bahamas, Caribbean.

SAW-BLADE ALGA   *Caulerpa serrulata*
SIZE: Blades ¾ - 1½ in.   Green Algae – Chlorophyta
ID: Small flattened blades with serrated edges grow upward from long, cylindrical runners. Blades often fork and twist. Mint green. Inhabit shallow rocky substrates. Occasional South Florida, Bahamas, Caribbean.

OVAL-BLADE ALGA   *Caulerpa prolifera*
SIZE: Blades 2 - 4 in.   Green Algae – Chlorophyta
ID: Small flat, elongated oval blades with short cylindrical stalks. Grow upward from long, cylindrical runners. Shades of green. Grow in sandy areas, often adjacent to shallow patch reefs. Occasional South Florida, Bahamas, Caribbean.

GREEN GRAPE ALGA
Caulerpa racemosa
Green Algae – Chlorophyta
SIZE: Height 1 - 6 in.
ID: Numerous long branching cylindrical runners bear clusters of grape-like spheres attached by tiny branchlets. Light to medium green, often with bluish tints. Most commonly grow in intertidal to shallow rocky areas, usually with at least some surge. Also inhabit rocky areas of shallow to moderately deep reefs. Common South Florida, Bahamas, Caribbean.

CACTUS TREE ALGA   *Caulerpa cupressoides*
SIZE: Height 1 - 10 in.   Green Algae – Chlorophyta
ID: Trunk-like stalks that divide into thick, heavy, upright branches extend from sand. Branches lined with rows of short, thick branchlets. Shades of green. Grow in shallow sandy areas. Occasional South Florida, Bahamas, Caribbean.

FUZZY FINGER ALGA   *Dasycladus vermicularis*
SIZE: Height 1 - 2½ in.   Green Algae – Chlorophyta
ID: Clusters of cylindrical branches composed of fine, tightly compacted branchlets. Olive to dark green. Grow in a variety of shallow water habitats attaching to hard substrates. Occasional South Florida, Bahamas, Caribbean.

DEAD MAN'S FINGERS   *Codium isthmocladum*
SIZE: Height 4 - 8 in.   Green Algae – Chlorophyta
ID: Bushy hemispherical growths of cylindrical branches with fine, hair-like covering. Often branch dichotomously near tips. Pale to medium green. Grow from shallow rocky substrates. Occasional South Florida, Bahamas, Caribbean.

SEA PEARL   *Valonia ventricosa*
SIZE: Diameter ¾ - 2 in.   Green Algae – Chlorophyta
ID: Dark green spheres with bright reflective sheen. Often covered with thin, silvery to light lavender algae. Often in small cracks in reefs. One of the world's largest single cells organisms. Common South Florida, Bahamas, Caribbean.

ELONGATED SEA PEARL   *Valonia macrophysa*
SIZE: Diameter ¼ - ¾ in.   Green Algae – Chlorophyta
ID: Dark green bubble-like cells with bright reflective, silvery sheen. Range from spheres to elongate ovals. Grow in tightly compacted, mat-like cluster in protected areas on reefs. Common South Florida, Bahamas, Caribbean.

CREEPING BUBBLE ALGA   *Valonia utricularis*
SIZE: Diameter ⅛ - ¼ in.   Green Algae – Chlorophyta
ID: Clusters of dark green, bubble-like cells grow in spreading runners. Do not from dense mats. Range from spheres to elongate ovals. Grow in protected areas on reefs. Occasional South Florida, Bahamas, Caribbean.

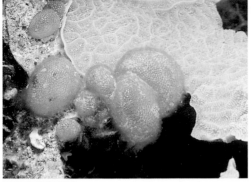

GREEN BUBBLE WEED   *Dictyosphaeria cavernosa*
SIZE: 1 - 8 in.   Green Algae – Chlorophyta
ID: Spherical to irregularly lobed clumps. Walls composed of small bubble-like cells giving surface a cobblestone-like texture. Shades of light green. Attach to rocky substrates and dead coral. Common South Florida, Bahamas, Caribbean.

PAPYRUS PRINT ALGA   *Anadyomene stellata*
SIZE: 1 - 4 in.   Green Algae – Chlorophyta
ID: Thin rounded, upright blades with long vertical veins that divide at tips into sprays of smaller veins, reminiscent of papyrus grass. Shades of green. Grow in shaded, protected areas. Occasional South Florida, Bahamas, Caribbean.

NETWORK ALGA
Microdictyon marinum
Green Algae – Chlorophyta
SIZE: 1 - 4 in.

ID: Clumps of thin stiff blades composed of compact network of long, rough filaments. Pale to dark green. Attach to hard substrate in open areas of reef. Often in environments with some light sedimentation. Occasional South Florida, Bahamas, Caribbean.

Green Algae

GREEN NET ALGA
Microdictyon umbilicatum
Green Algae – Chlorophyta
SIZE: 2 in. - 3 ft.
ID: Tangled masses formed by a somewhat stiff network of long, fine filaments. Pale to dark green. Grow in most marine environments; more common in areas with little water movement. May grow in small clumps or masses of considerable size covering large areas of substrate. Occasional Caribbean.

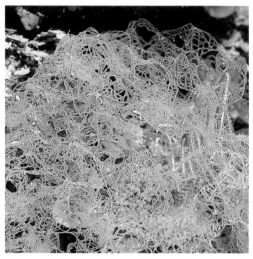

SAUCER BLADE ALGA   *Avrainvillea asarifolia*
SIZE: Height 2 - 6 in.   Green Algae – Chlorophyta
ID: Fan shaped blades with smooth edges and surface texture. Rounded bottom of blades turn in and upward toward stalks. Dark green. Grow in sandy areas on or between reefs. Common to occasional South Florida, Bahamas, Caribbean.

PADDLE BLADE ALGA   *Avrainvillea longicaulis*
SIZE: Height 2 - 4 in.   Green Algae – Chlorophyta
ID: Paddle-shaped blades with relatively smooth edges and surface texture. Stalks attached by large bulbous holdfast. Dark green. Grow in sandy areas on and between reefs. Common to occasional South Florida, Bahamas, Caribbean.

MERMAID'S FANS
Udotea spp.

Green Algae – Chlorophyta

SIZE: Height 1 - 8 in.

ID: Several species in this genus have broad, fan-shaped blades attached to a single stalk. Heavily calcified, stiff and erect. Whitish green to dark green. Because of similarity in appearance, species identification requires magnified examination of blade filaments. Grow in sandy, protected areas; usually in groups. Common South Florida, Bahamas, Caribbean.

MERMAID'S TEA CUP
Udotea cyathiformis

Green Algae – Chlorophyta

SIZE: Height 2 - 6 in.

ID: Paper-thin cup-shaped blade attaches to a small, single stalk anchored in sand. Quite delicate structure; easily torn. Medium green to whitish green. Typically grow in groups on sandy, protected areas. Occasional South Florida, Bahamas, Caribbean.

PINECONE ALGA
Rhipocephalus phoenix
Green Algae – Chlorophyta
SIZE: Height 2 - 5 in.
ID: Pinecone-shaped structure, composed of tightly-packed flattened blades growing upward and concentrically from a single stalk. Green to mint green and whitish green. Most frequently inhabit shallow sandy areas, including seagrass beds. Occasionally in sandy, rocky areas on and between reefs. Occasional South Florida, Bahamas, Caribbean.

WHITE MERMAID'S WINE GLASS   *Acetabularia crenulata*
SIZE: Cup diameter ¼ - ¾ in.   Green Algae – Chlorophyta
ID: Round, saucer-shaped caps on long, thin stalks. Ruffled rays radiate from centers, a small spine tips each ray. White with slight greenish tint. Grow in protected areas, singly or in groups. Occasional South Florida, Bahamas, Caribbean.

GREEN MERMAID'S WINE GLASS   *Acetabularia calyculus*
SIZE: Cup diameter ¼ - ½ in.   Green Algae – Chlorophyta
ID: Clumps of round, saucer-shaped caps on long thin stalks. Ruffled rays radiate from centers to edges. Pale green to yellowish green. Grow in shallow protected areas of reef and sand flats. Occasional South Florida, Bahamas, Caribbean.

TUBULAR THICKET ALGAE
Galaxaura spp.
Red Algae – Rhodophyta
SIZE: 4 - 6 in.
ID: Members of this genus cannot be distinguished visually. Segments branch dichotomously forming dense hemispherical domes attached by a single holdfast. Segments are tubular, smooth and relatively hard and heavily calcified; flexible joints. Tubular branch tips open at the end. Reddish to orangish white. Inhabit protected areas. Common to occasional Florida, Bahamas, Caribbean.

FLAT TWIG ALGA   *Amphiroa tribulus*
SIZE: 1 - 4 in.   Red Algae – Rhodophyta
ID: Grow in small tangled clumps. Randomly branched structures composed of thin, hard, flat segments. Flexible joints at forks. Whitish with pale red to pink tinting. Inhabit protected areas on reefs. Occasional Florida, Bahamas, Caribbean.

Y-TWIG ALGA   *Amphiroa rigida*
SIZE: 3 - 6 in.   Red Algae – Rhodophyta
ID: Grow in small tangled clumps of widely spaced, cylindrical, forked branches. Flexible obscure joints. Whitish often with pale red tint. Inhabit seagrass and protected areas of reefs. Occasional Florida, Bahamas, Caribbean.

225

Red Algae – Blue-green Algae

PINK SEGMENTED ALGA   *Jania adhaerens*
SIZE: 1 - 2 in.   Red Algae – Rhodophyta
ID: Grow in small tangled clumps. Wide, dichotomously branched structures composed of rigid, stony, cylindrical segments and flexible joints. Segments light red; joints white. Inhabit protected areas. Occasional Florida, Bahamas, Caribbean.

PINK BUSH ALGA   *Wrangelia penicillata*
SIZE: 4 - 8 in.   Red Algae – Rhodophyta
ID: Light pink color is distinctive of these bushy clumps. Small branches extend from main branches in a single plane. Grow in most marine environments. Attach to nearly any hard substrate. Common to occasional Florida, Bahamas, Caribbean.

REEF CEMENT

Red Algae – Rhodophyta
SIZE: Variable
ID: A number of species in several genera form thin hard, highly calcified encrustations overgrowing rocky limestone substrates. Take on contour of substrate. Shades of pinkish gray. Very important reef building element, acting as a cement-like covering and adhesive that protects the structure from destructive elements of strong surge and breaking waves. Often inside areas of clustered small holes bored by chitons. Abundant Florida, Bahamas, Caribbean.

LAVENDER CRUST ALGAE

Red Algae – Rhodophyta
SIZE: 1/2 - 1 in.
ID: Several indistinguishable species form thin, brittle encrustations on surfaces of many species of algae and seagrasses (pictured on Sea Pearls, *Valonia ventricosa*, [pg. 220]). Surface texture generally smooth, but occasionally covered with small knobby reproductive structures. Usually shades of grayish lavender. Abundant to occasional Florida, Bahamas, Caribbean.

CRUSTOSE CORALLINE ALGAE

Red Algae – Rhodophyta

SIZE: Plates 1 - 18 in.

ID: A number of species in several genera that generally form thin, brittle and highly calcified encrustations forming rounded plates. Dark red to burgundy, violet, lavender or pink, often with thin white margins. Extended edges of plates quite fragile. Prefer shaded areas of most marine habitats. Common Florida, Bahamas, Caribbean.

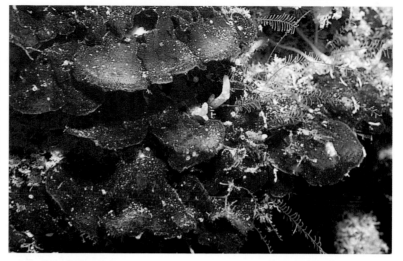

BURGUNDY CRUST ALGAE *Peyssonnelia* sp.

SIZE: 1 - 3 ft. Red Algae – Rhodophyta

ID: Thin, hard calcified encrusting growth taking on the contours of substrate. Dark red to burgundy. Prefer shaded areas, especially in cracks, along walls, caves and deep drop-offs. Abundant to occasional Florida, Bahamas, Caribbean.

FUZZ BALL ALGAE

SIZE: 1 - 3 in. Blue-green Algae – Cyanophyta

ID: Several species in this Phylum form fuzzy masses of filaments. Commonly dark burgundy to reddish tan. Prefer sunlit areas of shallow marine habitats. Often have no permanent holdfast. Common Florida, Bahamas, Caribbean.

Coral Health and Mortality

Recognizing the signs
of coral disease and predators

Compiled by Dr. Andrew Bruckner

Introduction

Throughout the western Atlantic, coral reefs have undergone dramatic changes as a consequence of human activity, natural disturbances, and a general deterioration of water quality. Hurricanes, disease and outbreaks of predators during the 1970s and 1980s transformed flourishing Elkhorn and Staghorn Coral thickets into fields of coral rubble and tissue-denuded skeletons still in growth position. From 1983-1984, a water-borne disease wiped out more than 90 percent of the population of the Caribbean's Long-spined Urchin, *Diadema antillarum*, that previously controlled algae – a major competitor of corals. This unprecedented die-off led to the widespread destruction of massive and plating corals at many sites throughout the region. The most significant localized factors leading to the degradation of coral reefs have been storms; an increase of sedimentation and nutrient run-off from land, rivers and sewage; overfishing; overgrowth by competing algae, sponges and tunicates; and outbreaks of coral predators. More recently, climate change has emerged as the largest global threat to coral reefs, with unprecedented increases in water temperature leading to mass bleaching events and outbreaks of coral disease.

Until the early 1990s, the only known coral diseases were White Band Disease, Black Band Disease and White Plague. The number of reported coral diseases and syndromes escalated during the mid-1990s. Today, coral diseases have now been documented to infect most common reef building corals in the Caribbean. Little is known about what causes these diseases, how a coral contracts them, and their potential long-term effects on reef systems. They may be caused by infectious pathogens, such as bacteria and fungi, a host of environmental stresses, such as elevated sea water temperatures and increased ultraviolet radiation, poor nutrition, genetic mutations (noninfectious diseases), or a combination of these and undetermined factors. Increased sedimentation, nutrients and pollutants may be responsible for an increase in pathogens or may decrease a coral's defense mechanisms and immune responses. Man's land-based activities are known to have introduced at least one coral disease, a soil fungus spread to seawater from river run-off that affects sea fans. A disease of Elkhorn Coral is thought to be caused by a pathogen in human sewage. Alarmingly, more and more reefs in unpopulated areas are also being affected by diseases, despite the absence of major human impacts in these areas.

A great deal of confusion exists about the nature of coral diseases because of factors such as incomplete designation of diseases and syndromes, as well as duplication of pathogen names and their causes or agents. Most coral diseases bear names that reflect the color of the diseased or affected tissues or the pattern of tissue loss. Over 50 names have been used by the scientific community to describe coral diseases. In some cases, different names have been given to the same disease and, in other cases, signs described as a disease may, in fact, be caused by coral predators. Further complicating matters, the appearance of a disease may vary according to depth, season or geographic location and coral colonies may be infected by more than one disease simultaneously.

Through the expansion of reef monitoring programs – many involving volunteer recreational divers – and improved laboratory techniques to investigate disease development and spread, coral disease and predators are being more fully understood, the purpose of this review is to help define a standard to better study coral diseases and predation.

A recent effort was undertaken by NOAA's Coral Disease and Health Consortium and the World Bank Coral Reef Targeted Research and Capacity Building for Management Program to standardize nomenclature and develop diagnostic criteria to identify and differentiate diseases. The initial assessment involves the identification of four easily observed descriptive categories: presence of color change, tissue loss, skeletal damage and/or irregular growth. The second step involves identifying the shape, location and distribution of the disease lesions. Further detail can be compiled on the texture, and characteristics of the margin between live, diseased and dead tissue. The categories are described below:

LESION DESCRIPTIONS:

Color Change – corals exhibiting change from their normal pigmentation or lack of pigmentation in tissues, typically exemplified by a white color.

Growth Anomaly – corals exhibiting excessive or apparently uncontrolled growth of skeleton or soft tissues in relation to adjacent polyps on the same colony; polyps may be deformed or normal in appearance but larger in size.

Skeletal Damage – structural damage to the skeleton associated with the abrasion and/or removal of the corallites and underlying skeletal layers; caused by fish bites, physical impacts, or environmental events.

Tissue Loss – corals manifesting absence of tissues with or without intact skeleton.

LESION SHAPE:

Annular – forming a ring.

Circular – forming a circle in appearance but larger in size.

Irregular – lacking symmetry; not straight, smooth, even, or regular.

Linear – forming a line.

Oblong – oval or elongate.

LESION DISTRIBUTION:

Coalescing – multiple lesions growing together.

Diffuse – not concentrated or localized.

Focal – central lesion surrounded by tissue.

Linear – beginning at the margin of the colony and advancing in a line or band.

Multifocal – multiple lesions within the colony surface, each surrounded by tissue.

LESION LOCATION:

Apical – situated near the apex or tip of the colony or branch.

Basal/Peripheral – situated near the base of the colony.

Central/Medial – lying or extending in the middle of the colony.

Healthy colony of Mountainous Star Coral.

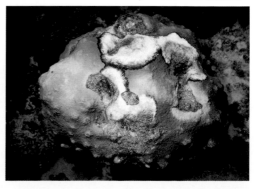
Mountainous Star Coral colony infected with disease.

Black Band Disease

VISUAL ID: Black Band Disease (BBD) is either crescent-shaped or a circular band of blackish filamentous material separating living, colored coral tissue from white, exposed skeleton. Over days to months BBD slowly spreads in a line across a colony, killing coral tissue as it advances. Infected areas can eventually expand to six feet (two meters) across. The bands are dark maroon to black due to the photosynthetic pigments (phycocyanin and phycoerythrin) of the cyanobacteria (blue-green algae). Bands often have a white dusting of filamentous (sulfide-oxidizing) bacteria. These microorganisms consist of long, unbranched filaments (visible to the naked eye) that are intertwined to form a dense mat. This mat is loosely anchored in living tissue and is easily dislodged by water movement.

Infections normally start at the fringe of a colony, in a surface depression or at the edge of a previous injury. Once BBD is established, it advances from a fraction of an inch to an inch (2 mm to 2 cm) per day. The disease is most apparent during phases of rapid advance, which generally occur when the water is clear and calm. During a brief period of a few days after a rapid advance begins, large portions of the white skeleton are exposed before a covering of green and brown filamentous algae becomes established and spreads over the area.

CORALS AFFECTED: In the western Atlantic, 24 species of common massive and plating corals, one hydrozoan coral and six gorgonians, including sea fans and branching sea rods, have been documented with BBD to date. The Boulder Star Coral, *Orbicella annularis*, and Symmetrical Brain Coral, *Pseudodiploria strigosa*, sustain the majority of infections. An additional 26 coral species in the Red Sea and Indo-Pacific are also affected. Staghorn Coral, *Acropora cervicornis*, and Elkhorn Coral, *A. palmata*, have not been observed with BBD.

CAUSE: Black Band Disease is a highly infectious disease caused primarily by a cyanobacteria (*Phormidium corallyticum*, *Geitlerinema* and other species, depending on location), in combination with sulfide oxidizing bacteria, *Beggiatoa* spp., and sulfur reducing bacteria, *Desulfovibrio* spp. Coral tissue is killed by the hydrogen sulfide produced by these microorganisms. Other opportunistic organisms such as ciliate protozoans, flatworms, nematodes, fungal filaments, and small crustaceans are also associated with the band. Bearded Fireworms, *Hermodice carunculata*, and coral-eating snails *Coralliophila* spp. are commonly seen feeding on tissue adjacent to the bands.

ABUNDANCE & DISTRIBUTION: BBD was first discovered on the reefs of Belize and Florida in 1972, and has since been identified on the coral reefs of 26 countries. The number of corals infected with BBD on a reef fluctuates, but BBD is always present at some level, to depths of just over 100 feet. In the late summer and early fall, when water is clear and calm and temperatures reach their peak, colonies become far more susceptible to infection and the rapid spread of the disease. BBD disappears, or becomes more difficult to find, when water temperatures drop below 72 F (22 C). The disease also subsides during extended periods of low water visibility. BBD is uncommon in areas of high wave action.

IMPACT: Research has been conducted in Belize, Florida, Jamaica, Puerto Rico and the Virgin Islands to understand more about the distribution, abundance and impact of BBD. Typically, a few corals show signs of this disease on any particular reef during its active season. In a few locations up to 50 percent of coral colonies can be affected. Small colonies may be killed by BBD in weeks to months, but relatively few of the larger corals die from a single infection event. In most cases, a colony loses up to half of its tissue before the disease disappears. Unfortunately, colonies are occasionally reinfected. Partial tissue loss affects a coral's ability to reproduce. Also, the portion of a coral killed is often colonized by organisms such as boring sponges that erode the skeleton, further limiting the colony's ability to recover.

Symmetrical Brain Coral infected with Black Band Disease. [right]

Spread of Black Band Disease over two week period. [middle]

Blushing Star Coral infected with Black Band Disease. [bottom left]

Bearded Fireworm feeding on coral tissue adjacent to diseased band. [bottom right]

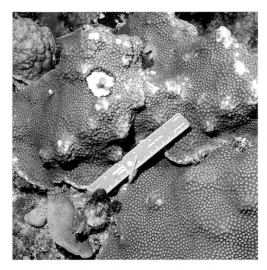

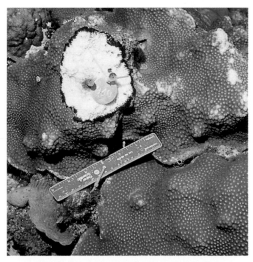

White Band Disease

VISUAL ID: Typically White Band Disease (WBD), which affects branching corals, starts at the base of a colony and progresses toward branch tips, but occasionally it begins in the middle of a colony, especially at the points where branches begin. Unlike BBD, there is no obvious black mat; instead, colonies affected by WBD display a margin of slowly advancing tissue decay, which exposes a contrasting bright white area of limestone skeleton next to dying tissue. The disease causes tissue to peel away from the skeleton at a fairly uniform rate of just under a quarter inch (5 mm) per day, although the disease can advance much more rapidly. The exposed skeleton, varying from a fraction of an inch to four inches wide (a few millimeters to 10 cm) is colonized by algae in a matter of days. An entire colony rarely suffers complete mortality; however, recovered colonies are often reinfected.

CORALS AFFECTED: Staghorn Coral, *Acropora cervicornis,* Elkhorn Coral, *A. palmata,* and Fused Staghorn Coral, *A. prolifera.*

CAUSE: No definitive cause has been identified for WBD; however, a host of bacteria, fungi and protozoans are often found at the site of infection. Rod-shaped, bacteria-like organisms have been identified within the coral tissue of some infected colonies, but these also occur in corals that appear healthy.

ABUNDANCE & DISTRIBUTION: WBD was first observed in 1977 on reefs surrounding St. Croix, USVI. It has since been identified throughout the wider Caribbean and in Red Sea, Indo-Pacific, and the Gulf of Oman. Although WBD only affects acroporids on Caribbean reefs, the same, or a similar disease, has been observed on several other genera in the Indo-Pacific. The signs of WBD are similar to White Plague, a disease that affects Caribbean corals other than Staghorn Coral and Elkhorn Coral. In the Caribbean, the incidence of WBD ranges from less than one percent to 64 percent of the colonies in a single area. WBD epizootics (the equivalent of an epidemic in humans) were first reported throughout the Caribbean in the late 1970s and again in 1980s and 1990s. The disease is still common today; however, it may be less conspicuous because of a marked decline of the three species of *Acropora* and because of confusion with a similar disease that also affects the same coral species (see below).

IMPACT: White Band Disease is believed to be the major factor responsible for the widespread decline of Caribbean acroporid corals in the 1980s. Mass mortalities have led to a virtual elimination of Staghorn and Elkhorn thickets from shallow reef environments throughout the region. For example, large stands of Elkhorn Coral that were formerly abundant in the USVI (St. Croix) declined from 85 percent cover to 5 percent within 10 years. White Band Disease is the first coral disease documented to have caused major changes in the composition and structure of reefs.

Related White Syndromes

VISUAL ID: A second form of White Band Disease, known as White Band Disease Type II, was first identified in the Bahamas in 1993. WBD II is believed to be more virulent, causing tissue death at a much more rapid rate. The disease spreads from the base of a colony toward the branch tips. It appears as a band of bleached tissue varying from just less than one inch to eight inches (2 to 20 cm) wide that separates the normal pigmented tissue from the white dead skeleton. A bacteria of the genus *Vibrio*, which lives on the surface mucus of the bleached tissue, may cause WBD II. This condition appears to have become much more common over the last decade among Staghorn Coral colonies, and can cause total colony mortality in a few days time.

White Patch Disease (WPD), formerly called White Pox (POX) and Patchy Necrosis (PN), also affect Elkhorn Coral and Staghorn Coral. This disease is easily distinguished from WBD. The disease manifests as small patches of dead tissue that are surrounded completely by normal tissue, in contrast to the prominent linear bands of tissue decay associated with WBD. Patches are most frequently located on the upper surfaces of branches.

White Patch Disease was first reported from Puerto Rico in 1994 and from the Florida Keys during 1996, but is now believed to occur throughout the Caribbean. The disease starts as small, circular white spots or irregular patches from less than an inch to four inches (2 to 10 cm) in diameter on the upper or lower surfaces of the branches. The numerous white patches are bare of coral tissue. Once infected, the patches expand rapidly. In some cases they eventually cause a colony's death. More frequently, the patch size increases rapidly for a few days, then the spread slows markedly and eventually stops. As with other diseases, colonies may be reinfected in new locations. After several infectious events, Elkhorn branches are a mosaic of live tissue interspersed with white, recently killed areas and older lesions. The disease is less common during winter months, and often tissue will resheet over old lesions.

A bacteria found in the human gut that has been transmitted to the reef via sewage discharge has been identified as the possible cause for the disease in the Florida Keys. There is also evidence that similar patterns of tissue loss in Elkhorn Coral are caused by repeated biting by the Threespot Damselfish, *Stegastes planifrons*, and the Yellowtail Damselfish, *Microspathodon chrysurus*.

Staghorn Coral infected with White Band Disease. [middle left] *Elkhorn Coral infected with White Patch Disease.* [middle right] *Elkhorn Coral infected with White Patch Disease.* [bottom left] *Damselfish biting on Elkhorn Coral.* [bottom left]

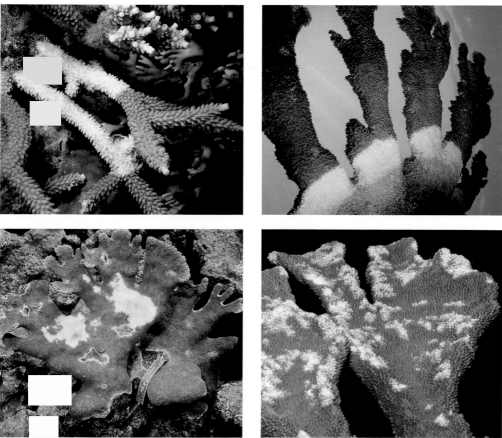

White Plague

VISUAL ID: White Plague (WP), which is similar in appearance to White Band Disease, affects massive and plating corals. Tissue loss begins at the base or margin of a colony, or next to a previously diseased area, and quickly spreads. A sharp line separates healthy tissue from the bare skeleton; however there is no visible mat of organisms at the disease front. A fine, but distinct, narrow band of bleached tissue may separate normal, fully pigmented tissue from the white, exposed skeleton. Tissue loss progresses up to 3/4 of an inch (2 cm) per day.

Two forms of White Plague have been described: White Plague Type I, which was documented in the 1970s and 1980s, and White Plague Type II first reported in the mid-1990s from the same reefs in Florida. The disease signs of both forms are similar, and there is some overlap of affected species. However, in White Plague Type II the disease spreads rapidly, with the ability to kill a small coral in just one to two days; White Plague Type I advances only a few millimeters each day and can take from 3 to 4 months to kill an entire colony. Elliptical Star Coral, *Dichocoenia stokesi*, a species never observed with WP in the 1970s or 1980s, appears particularly vulnerable to White Plague Type II.

CORALS AFFECTED: At least 13 species of massive and plating corals are affected by White Plague Type I, primarily Starlet Coral, *Siderasterea* spp., Cactus Corals, *Mycetophyllia* spp., and Boulder Brain Coral, *Colpophyllia natans*; 40 species are affected by White Plague Type II. It does not affect Staghorn Coral, *Acropora cervicornis* or Elkhorn Coral, *A. palmata*.

CAUSE: White Plague Type II is caused by a rod-shaped bacterium, *Aurantimonas coralicida*. Several bacteria were found to live in association with White Plague Type I, but have never been confirmed as the cause of the disease.

ABUNDANCE & DISTRIBUTION: WP was first described from the Florida Keys in 1977 on Starlet Coral, Cactus Coral and Boulder Brain Coral. In the 1980s it was also observed on Mountainous Star Coral, *Orbicella faveolata*. Outbreaks have been reported from Puerto Rico and the USVI, and many other locations. White Plague Type II emerged during 1995 in the Florida Keys, initially attacking the Elliptical Star Coral, *Dichocoenia stokesi*, a coral previously presumed to be resistant to diseases. Due to the rapid advance of this disease, small corals are killed within a few days. Outbreaks of White Plague among large colonies of Mountainous Star Corals and brain corals were reported from around the Caribbean in the spring and summer of 2001, with colonies more than a meter in diameter being killed in about a week. More severe outbreaks have been documented following mass bleaching events in 2005 (Puerto Rico and the US Virgin Islands), 2009 (Cayman Islands) and 2010-2011 (Bonaire, Colombia).

IMPACT: In an extensive study conducted in the Florida Keys in the 1970s, involving nearly 10,000 coral colonies, up to 73 percent of corals on some sites were found to be infected with White Plague Type I. White Plague Type II spread throughout the Florida Keys between 1995 and 1998, with the highest number of infections on Elliptical Star Corals (up to 38 percent were affected on some reefs), many died within days of becoming infected. Nearly half of the brain corals on one reef in Puerto Rico were affected in 1996; fortunately most suffered only partial mortality and the disease has since declined in abundance. More recently (2005-2010), White Plague has contributed to a region-wide decline of Lobed Star Coral, *Orbicella annularis*, with living coral cover declining in some locations from 30-50% to 5-10%. Among this genus, colonies that were several meters in diameter and height, and 100s of years old, were completely killed within about a month.

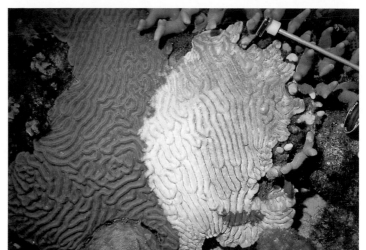

Boulder Brain Coral infected with White Plague Type I. The disease can kill an entire colony in two to three months.

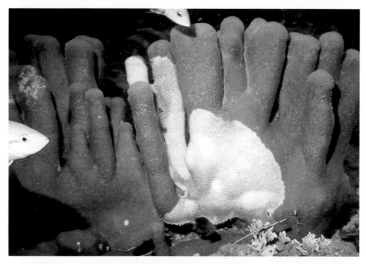

Pillar Coral infected with White Plague Type II. The disease spreads very rapidly and can kill an entire small colony in one to two days!

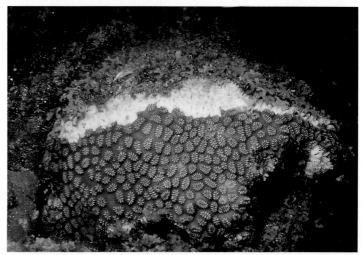

Elliptical Star Coral was never observed with White Plague in the 1970s or 1980s, but now appears to be particularly vulnerable to White Plague Type II.

Caribbean Yellow Band Disease

VISUAL ID: Caribbean Yellow Band Disease (CYBD) begins as a pale yellow, circular blotch of tissue in the middle of a colony or as a narrow band at the edge of a colony. Infected areas are surrounded by normal, dark green to brown tissue. Affected tissue is translucent, but still contains a reduced number of symbiotic algae (zooxanthellae). As the pale yellow leading edge of CYBD advances, tissue adjacent to the exposed skeleton gradually darkens and dies. The band advances up to 3/8 of an inch (1 cm) per month. Because the spread is relatively slow, colonies rarely have a prominent area of white, exposed skeleton. Typically, tissue mortality is restricted to small one- to four-square-inch (5-10 cm) irregular blotches. Colonies affected by CYBD can be identified during bleaching events by the presence of a characteristic annular or linear band that is pale yellow in color, but darker than surrounding bleached tissue. These areas do not appear to bleach, even though the remainder of the colony may be stark white in color. Multiple lesions may occur on a single colony. Over time these coalesce and continue expanding. Although the rate of tissue loss is much slower than other coral diseases, an infection can exist for years, eventually killing large colonies.

CORALS AFFECTED: Lobed, Mountainous and Boulder Star Corals, *Orbicella annularis, O. faveolata* and *O. franksi*, are most frequently affected, but also reported on Great Star Coral, *Montastraea cavernosa*, and Boulder Brain Coral, *Colpophyllia natans*.

CAUSE: CYBD is associated with several species of *Vibrio* bacteria. This condition has been confused with bleaching and has been incorrectly referred to as "Ring Bleaching." It was previously known as "Yellow Blotch Disease."

ABUNDANCE & DISTRIBUTION: Caribbean Yellow Band Disease was first identified in 1994 in the Florida Keys, and has since been reported from Curacao, Bonaire, Panama, Mexico and Puerto Rico.

IMPACT: Monitoring efforts for CYBD in the Caribbean have recorded an increased incidence, accompanied by alarming coral mortality in the late 1990s. The disease kills coral tissue at a rate of 3 to 6 inches (7-15 cm) per year, which is considerably slower than the rate observed for other diseases. However, corals become infected in many locations and infections persist for several years. CYBD appears to be particularly common on the largest and oldest corals found on a reef. In a specific area, up to 50 percent of boulder-type corals may be infected.

Caribbean Yellow Band Disease begins as a pale yellow to white blotch [below] or band [below right].

As the disease advances the tissue behind the narrow pale blotch or band darkens to a yellowish brown and eventually dies.

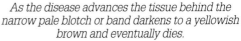

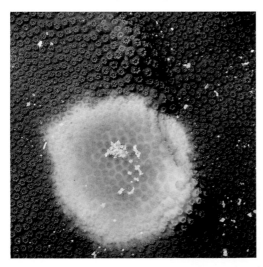

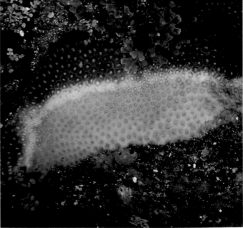

Caribbean Yellow Band Disease infected Great Star Coral [right], *Boulder Star Coral* [below middle left] *Symmetrical Brain Coral.* [below middle right]

Caribbean Yellow Band Disease spreads much slower than other coral diseases, but none-the-less will eventually kill an entire colony. Mountainous Star Coral colony in August 1999. [bottom left] *and the same colony May 2001.* [bottom right]

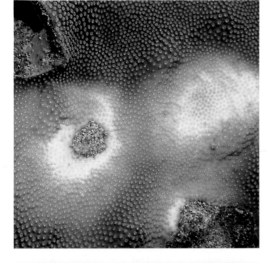

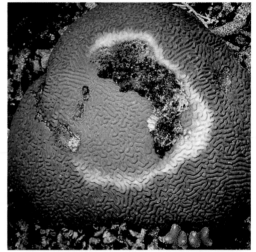

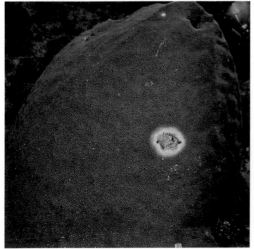

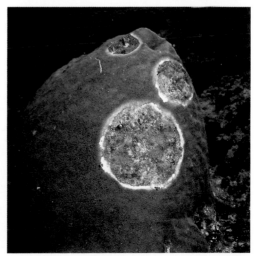

Red Band Disease

VISUAL ID: Red Band Disease (RBD) consists of a narrow band or line of filamentous cyanobacteria (blue-green algae) that advances slowly across the surface of a coral killing living tissue as it advances. There are two types of RBD, referred to as RBD-1 and RBD-2.

RBD-1, like Black Band Disease, it forms a distinct band that separates living coral tissue from bare white skeleton as it advances a few millimeters each day. Unlike BBD, the band is red to maroon and the cyanobacterial filaments are often more loosely organized and less mat-like.

RBD-2 is visibly different from RBD-1. During daylight, the filaments spread like a net over a colony's surface. At night the band forms a compact "balled-up" mat at the interface between the living tissue and the exposed skeleton.

CORALS AFFECTED: RBD-1 infects Lettuce Corals, *Agaricia* spp., Boulder Brain Coral, *Colpophyllia natans*, Cactus Corals, *Mycetophyllia* spp., Blushing Star Coral, *Stephanocoenia intersepta*, and the Common Seafan, *Gorgonia ventalina*.

RBD-2 infects Symmetrical Brain Coral, *Pseudodiplioria strigosa*, the Lobed, Mountainous and Boulder Star Corals, *Orbicella annularis, O. faveolata* and *O. franksi*, Great Star Coral, *Montastraea cavernosa*, Mustard Hill Coral, *Porites astreoides*, and Massive Starlet Coral, *Siderastrea siderea*.

CAUSE: Based on the structure of microscopic filaments from Belize, RBD appears to be caused by at least two species of cyanobacteria: *Schizothrix* and *Spirulina*. However, an examination of the genetic structure of RBD-1 cyanobacteria (using 16s RNA) indicates that they may be more closely related to other cyanobacteria (*Oscillatoria* and the *Gloeotheca-Gloecapsa*). Two species of *Oscillatoria* were observed in RBD-2 samples from the Bahamas.

ABUNDANCE AND DISTRIBUTION: RBD-1 was first observed on sea fans during 1983 in Belize. RBD has also been observed in the Bahamas, Curacao, Puerto Rico and Jamaica. RBD-2 was first reported in the early 1990s in the Bahamas. It now occurs throughout the Caribbean at a low prevalence, primarily among *Agaricia*. No information is available on the abundance or impact of RBD.

Common Sea Fan infected with Red Band Disease Type 1.

Cactus Coral infected with Red Band Disease Type 1. The disease closely resembles Black Band Disease, but is red to maroon, rather than black to dark maroon, and is also generally more filamentous.

Lettuce Coral infected with Red Band Disease Type 1; note the filamentous band.

Boulder Star Coral infected with Red Band Disease Type 2. The filaments spread like a net over the colony's surface.

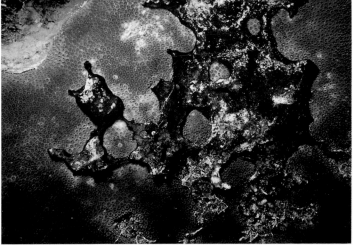

Dark Spots Diseases

VISUAL ID: Dark Spots Disease (DSD) appears as circular to irregular areas of pale discolored tissue with darkened polyps or spots in the middle of normal tissue or at the colony's margin. Discolored tissue spreads as the affected tissue dies. On Massive Starlet Coral discolored areas may be pink, brown, or blue, although colonies with a bluish hue may be showing signs of bleaching. In a few instances, most noticeably on Blushing Star Coral, the darkened polyps are slightly depressed and smaller than normal polyps. Some researchers have subdivided DSD into several types, including DSD type II, purple band syndrome and tissue necrosis. Each of these conditions shares similarities to DSD type I, although the coloration, distribution of lesions and patterns of tissue loss may vary.

CORAL AFFECTED: DSD is most commonly observed on Massive Starlet Coral, *Siderastrea siderea*, and Blushing Star Coral, *Stephanocoenia intersepta*, but has also been reported on Lobed, Mountainous and Boulder Star Corals, *Orbicella annularis, O. faveolata* and *O. franski*, Lettuce Coral, *Agaricia* spp. and pencil corals, *Madracis* spp.

CAUSE: The cause of DSD is unknown. A bacteria (*Vibrio carchariae*) has been found in association with DSD.

ABUNDANCE & DISTRIBUTION: First reported from Colombia during the late 1990s. This condition now occurs on reefs throughout the Caribbean. In some corals it appears seasonally, disappearing during winter months. An unusually high abundance of affected lettuce coral and cactus corals were identified in 2010-2011 in the Cayman Islands and Bahamas. Little information is available on its impact.

*Blushing Star Coral
infected with Dark Spots Disease.*

*Massive Starlet Coral infected
with Dark Spots Disease.*

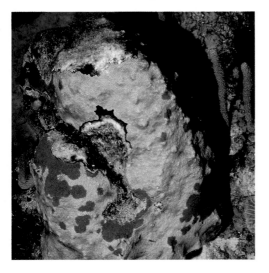

Irregular Growths:
Hyperplasm and Neoplasm (Tumors)

VISUAL ID: A hyperplasm is an area of accelerated growth of coral polyps. It results in corallite distortion and other malformations. Ridges and valleys on brain corals, or circular polyps in star corals are enlarged and project above the colony surface. Polyps are visible but appear exaggerated.

Coral Disease

A neoplasm is an irregular, calcified mass of skeleton that projects above the surface of the colony. It is covered with undifferentiated tissue that lacks symbiotic algae and the structural organization of normal tissue that makes individual polyps unrecognizable. Certain cells within the neoplasm (calicoblastic epithelial cells) grow and multiply at a rapid rate causing a progressive increase in the size of the tumor. This condition may slowly advance upward and outward as tissue in the center of the tumor dies.

CORALS AFFECTED: All corals are believed to be susceptible to both types. Neoplasm generally affects Elkhorn Coral, *Acropora palmata*.

CAUSE: Some tumors may form in response to algal and fungal agents, or certain stresses such as high ultraviolet radiation, while others may be genetic mutations.

ABUNDANCE & DISTRIBUTION: Abnormal/irregular growths on corals were first reported over 30 years ago. These conditions appear to be widespread, but their abundance and impact are unknown.

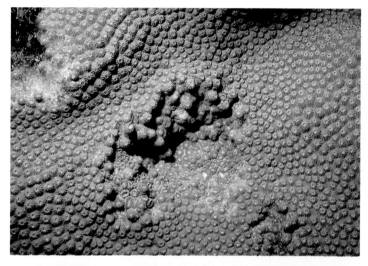

Mountainous Star Coral infected with Hyperplasm Tumors. [right]

Boulder Brain Coral infected with Hyperplasm Tumors. [bottom left]

Elkhorn Coral infected with Neoplasm Tumor. [bottom right]

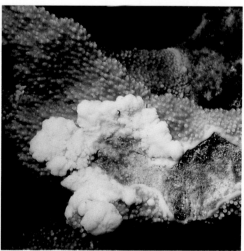

Coral Health and Mortality
Caribbean Ciliate Infections

VISUAL ID: Caribbean Ciliate Infection (CCI) can show two distinct patterns: a diffuse black or gray band, several mm to 2 cm thick, separating healthy tissue from bare skeleton or a diffuse scattered patch. Both bands and patches have a "salt-and-pepper" speckled appearance caused by the presence of ciliates. Patches may be associated with colonizing algae on bare skeleton. Ciliates may also be secondary colonizers on corals recovering from white plague and white band disease.

CORALS AFFECTED: CCI is known to infect more than 25 species of hard corals in six families (Acroporidae, Agaricidae, Astrocoeniidae, Faviidae, Meandrinidae and Poritidae).

CAUSE: CCI is caused by a folliculinid ciliate in the genus *Hallofoliculina*.

ABUNDANCE & DISTRIBUTION: The disease was first observed off the Caribbean coast of Venezuela, Colombia and Mexico during 2004-2005 but it is now known to be Caribbean-wide CCI appears to be more common in offshore oceanic reefs rather than coastal, human-influenced reefs.

IMPACT: Unknown; no outbreaks have been reported. Tissue loss is fairly slow (about 0.8 cm per month.

Banded pattern of Caribbean Ciliate Infection on Staghorn Coral, Acropora cervicornis.

Patch pattern of Caribbean Ciliate Infection on Mountainous Star Coral, Orbicella faveolata.

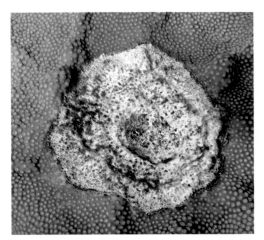

Patch pattern of Caribbean Ciliate Infection on Elkhorn Coral, Acropora palmata.

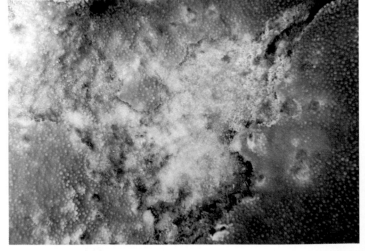

Coral Bleaching

VISUAL ID: Bleaching results in the loss of the symbiotic algae (zooxanthellae) contained within coral tissue, or as a reduction of the photosynthetic pigments of the zooxanthellae that give the coral its normal color. In either case, the coral appears lighter in color, mottled or white. In some species, such as Massive Starlet Coral, *Siderastrea siderea,* partially bleached colonies may be a shade of blue or pink.

CORALS AFFECTED: All species are susceptible; certain species are more resistant, except under extreme conditions.

CAUSE: Bleaching may be caused by a wide range of environmental stresses, but is most commonly caused by elevated water temperatures and increased ultraviolet radiation especially during El Niño events and doldrum-like conditions associated with prolonged periods of clear water and flat seas. Localized bleaching also occurs when corals are exposed to extremes in salinity, pollution, increased sedimentation, or unusually low temperatures. In a few cases, *Vibrio* bacteria and protozoans have been known to cause bleaching.

ABUNDANCE & DISTRIBUTION: Coral bleaching of single corals has been observed on coral reefs for over 100 years, but only recently have mass bleaching events been recorded. Most coral bleaching events are extremely localized with only certain colonies on a particular reef affected. The intensity of bleaching, number of species affected, distribution of bleached corals, and amount of mortality caused by bleaching has varied considerably among reefs and years. However, bleaching events appear to have increased in intensity, frequency and geographic distribution in the past two decades and bleaching events over the last 15 years have been associated with widespread coral die-offs. Nine major episodes of temperature-related bleaching have occurred since 1979, with the most severe region-wide event in 1998 and severe localized events in 2005 (Puerto Rico, USVI and Eastern Caribbean), 2009 (Cayman Islands) and 2010 (Bonaire, Curacao).

IMPACT: Without symbiotic algae, which provide corals with their major source of energy, bleached corals are under increased stress. In most circumstances, corals recover fully from bleaching, but recovery takes several months with some colonies experiencing partial tissue loss. If stresses are prolonged, most, if not all, of a coral's polyps die. Bleached corals are more susceptible to coral diseases. During post bleaching recovery periods following the 2005, 2009 and 2010 events, widespread outbreaks of white plague were documented.

Bleached colony of Great Star Coral.   *Bleached colony of Yellow Pencil Coral.*

Coral Health and Mortality

Bleaching does not affect all colonies, even of the same species uniformly. Side by side bleached and not bleached colonies of Maze Coral. [left]

Bleaching Colonies
Thin Leaf Lettuce Coral. [middle left]
Boulder Star Coral. [middle right]
Lobed Star Coral. [bottom left]
Symmetrical Brain Coral. [bottom right]

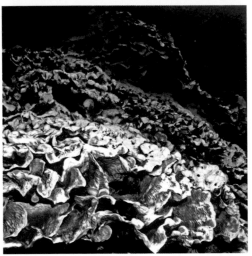

Massive bleaching event of sheet corals on wall in Bonaire in 1998. [right]

Severely bleached colony of White Star Sheet Coral. [bottom left]

Under some circumstances, corals can recover from bleaching. Same colony fully recovered several months later. [bottom right]

However, if the stresses that caused bleaching are prolonged most if not all of the coral polyps die.

Gorgonian Diseases

VISUAL ID: Reports of disease on octocorals have increased in recent years. At least three diseases are now known to affect Caribbean Sea Fans, *Gorgonia* spp. Black Band Disease (BBD) and Red Band Disease (RBD) were first observed in 1982, while a third disease, Aspergillosis, was reported in 1996. Octocorals are also affected by tumors and various invertebrate predators, and may also be overgrown by Fire Corals, *Millepora* spp.

BBD affects sea fans and the Sea Plumes, *Antillogorgia* spp., while RBD has only been observed on sea fans. Both RBD and BBD start at the base of a colony, or within the blade at sites of previous injuries. The disease forms a characteristic band, 1-20 mm wide that progressively advances outward as it kills sea fan tissue. Once the tissue is dead, the skeleton quickly becomes fouled with sediment and algae.

Aspergillosis caused by a soil fungus, *Aspergillus* spp., results in the death of tissue and erosion of the skeleton. Common Sea Fan, *Gorgonia ventalina,* and the Venus Sea Fan, *G. flabellum,* display one or more irregular patches that lack living tissue. These areas expand in size until they eventually result in holes in the blades. The living tissue surrounding these lesions often becomes dark purple and may develop spherical nodules or galls (tumors). Many sea fans often have similar-appearing lesions, dark areas and tumors that have no association with Aspergillosis. The disease can only be verified by the presence of fine white fungal filaments adjacent to living tissue, that is extremely difficult to detect in the field with the naked eye.

Sea fans are commonly observed with dark purple, round or oblong growths or nodules (tumors) on the main branches or on the blade. These tumors can increase in size and number and spread over a colony, and may result in tissue death and erosion of the skeleton.

Sea fans commonly have tumors that appear as dark purple, round or oblong nodules that with growth may result in tissue death and erosion of the fan's skeleton.

Sea Fan infected with Red Band Disease. The infection usually starts at the bottom of the colony and spreads upward eventually killing the cntirc colony.

Aspergillosis is a fungus infection attacking sea fans. The infection kills patches of tissue, ultimately causing holes in the fan.

Branching Fire Coral often overgrows sea fans and other gorgonians.

Gorgonian Predators

Several species of snails feed on gorgonians including Flamingo Tongue, *Cyphoma gibbosum*, and Coral Snail, *Coralliophila* spp. These snails typically graze a trail across the gorgonian as they consume tissue. Grazing trails occasionally expose the spicules (skeletal elements in the colony's structure) in a line the width of the predators' bodies. The other coral-eating snails, *Coralliophila* spp., typically remain close to the holdfast and are more difficult to detect. They often feed in small clusters on a sea fan or sea plume leaving characteristic feeding scars that extend up the blade in narrow lines. The Bearded Fireworm, *Hermodice carunculata*, is also a common gorgonian predator commonly feeding on Deep Water Sea Fans, *Iciligorgia schrammi*, and other gorgonians.

Bearded Fireworms regularly feed on Deep Water Sea Fans and other gorgonians.
[right]

Detail of gorgonian tissue damage from feeding Flamingo Tongue.
[below left]

Flamingo Tongues regularly feed on Regal Sea Fans and other gorgonians.
[below right]

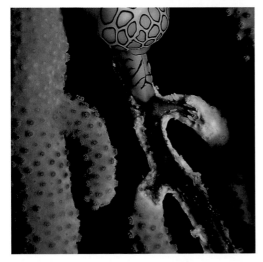

*An infestation of adult and juvenile
Flamingo Tongues ravages a bushy gorgonian.* [top]

A pair of adult Flamingo Tongues feed on a sea rod. [below right]
*Juvenile Flamingo Tongue
feeds on Deep Water Sea Fan.* [below left]

Bearded Fireworm Predation
Hermodice carunculata

VISUAL ID: Bearded Fireworms prey on most species of corals, but appear to have a preference for branching corals and corals that have been weakened by disease. They feed primarily on branch tips of Staghorn Coral, *Acropora cervicornis*, on raised knobs on Elkhorn Coral, *Acropora palmata*, and on fire coral, *Millepora* spp. Damage caused by worms is very conspicuous, but feeding behavior may not be observed as worms primarily feed at night. Bearded Fireworm damage can be differentiated from disease by its location near branch tips; diseases affecting this species generally spread from the base toward branch tips.

Short Coral Snail
Coralliophila abbreviata

VISUAL ID: The Short Coral Snail, *Coralliophila abbreviata*, is found on over 20 species of stony corals and occasionally on soft corals. Small aggregations of up to 20 snails regularly cluster together. The snails are rarely noticed because of a camouflage of algal growth. Smaller snails tend to live at the base of the colony, or under flattened plates near the periphery of dead tissue. They emerge to feed at night. Larger snails will aggregate in the open on branches of Elkhorn Coral, and occasionally on other species, where they create prominent grazing scars.

CORALS AFFECTED: Elkhorn Coral, *Acropora palmata*, Staghorn Coral, *A. cervicornis*, Massive Starlet Coral, *Siderastrea siderea* and Lettuce Coral, *Agaricia agaricites*, but snails are most common on Lobed Star Coral, *Orbicella annularis* where hundreds of animals may gather between the lobes. Snail predation may be confused with White Syndromes, but can be easily distinguished by its scalloped pattern matching the shape and size of the predatory snails.

ABUNDANCE & DISTRIBUTION: In Florida and Puerto Rico, large snails are unusually common on Elkhorn Coral possibly because corals are scarcer and populations of the Caribbean Spiny Lobster, *Panulirus argus*, their historic predators, have been overharvested.

IMPACT: In general, corals sustain small amounts of predation by snails, especially the branching corals that grow at relatively fast rates. However, because these snails can aggregate in large numbers and can grow quite large (up to about 2 inches [5 cm] in length), they occasionally kill entire colonies.

Bearded Fireworm feeding on Orange Cup Coral.

Bearded Fireworm feeding on Staghorn Coral; note living tissue has been stripped from branch tip.

The shells of Short Coral Snails are well camouflaged with algal growth; note five individuals in the picture. [far left]

Short Coral Snails clustered near the base of Elkhorn Coral colony. [left]

Coral Predation

Predation of stony corals by coral eating animals (corallivores) is much less prevalent in the Caribbean than in the Indo-Pacific. These can be divided into three main categories: excavators, scrapers, and browsers/grazers. Excavators remove coral tissue and a substantial portion of the underlying skeleton, while scrapers remove tissue and only the upper surfaces of the coral calices. Browsers and grazers typically remove soft parts without significantly damaging the skeleton. Some invertebrates also feed exclusively on coral mucus, without causing gross visible lesions.

Of the 35 known Caribbean corallivores, only two invertebrates can cause significant damage, coral snails, *Coralliophila* spp., and the Bearded Fireworm, *Hermodice carunculata*. Urchins erode the coral surface to form shallow depressions (home cavities), but they will also abrade coral tissue, especially when their population density increases and food (algae) becomes overgrazed. In the Caribbean, both *Diadema antillarum* and *Echinometra viridis* can erode corals to create burrows, bioeroding coral skeleton and abrading living coral tissue. Other minor invertebrate corallivores are the Coral Snail *Coralliophila caribea*, the Green Clinging Crab, *Mithrax sculptus*, Top Shells, *Calliostoma* spp., and the gastropod *Pedicularia decussata*. There are also 19 species of fish that feed on coral. Parrotfish (*Scaridae*), pufferfish, triggerfish, filefish, wrasses, and most damselfish are either scrapers or excavators, and have the ability to remove a considerable amount of skeletal material along with coral tissue. Damselfish, *Pomacentridae*, can also pick at the coral, removing only tissue with no obvious visible underlying skeletal damage. Butterflyfish, *Chaetodontidae*, exhibit diverse feeding strategies: some selectively browse individual coral polyps, some graze coral colonies removing tissue and skeleton, and others feed primarily on mucus, causing minimal damage to live tissue. Damselfish can kill entire colonies as they create their algal lawns. Only the Stoplight Parrotfish, *Sparisoma viride*, consumes large amounts of living coral tissue, primarily star corals and Boulder Brain Coral, *Colpophyllia natans*.

With the exception of fireworms and the coral snails, both of which can cause conspicuous damage, the majority of invertebrates cause little obvious damage to their host. The only known large-scale coral mortality associated with invertebrate predation occurred in Jamaica, when Staghorn Coral, *Acropora cervicornis*, failed to recover after corallivores concentrated on the few remaining living colonies and fragments following hurricane destruction.

Parrotfish Focused Biting

VISUAL ID: Several parrotfish, including the Queen, *Scarus vetula,* Stoplight, *Sparisoma viride,* Rainbow, *Scarus guacamaia* and Redband, *Scarus aurofrenatum* frequently feed on live coral. These fish typically take numerous small bites, called "Spot Biting," over the surface of coral heads creating obvious paired grazing scars. Large female and male Stoplight Parrotfish often return repeatedly to bite the same area of a coral head, producing large obvious lesions on the colony's surface. These lesions spread progressively across the coral, but rarely kill an entire colony completely. This behavior, called Focused Biting, has been incorrectly referred to as "Rapid Wasting Disease." Signs of fish predation are distinct from signs of disease. Damage caused by fish bites generally removes both living tissue and the top layers of the skeleton, whereas disease leaves the coral skeleton intact.

Focused biting caused by Stoplight Parrotfishes is observed most frequently on Lobed Star Coral, *Orbicella annularis,* Mountainous Star Coral, *O. faveolata,* and Boulder Brain Coral, *Colpophyllia natans,* although most stony corals are occasionally bitten as well. Affected colonies appear to have been physically abraded, with damage extending in one- to four-inch (2 to 10 cm) wide strips. Fish characteristically remove tissue and skeleton from the top portions of a single lobe of star corals, before beginning the same behavior on an adjacent, previously undamaged lobe. The process is repeated for days to weeks until multiple lobes on an individual colony are damaged. Parrotfish bite at prominent knobs or projections on Mountainous Star Coral leaving golf ball-sized, or larger, lesions. Boulder Brain Coral grazing usually begins at the colony's edge and methodically progresses forming a uniform strip. Plating- and branching-type corals are usually bitten around their edges and branch tips. An extensive release of coral mucus is often associated with recent bite marks.

ABUNDANCE & DISTRIBUTION: Parrotfish predation on coral was first reported over 100 years ago. It can be observed on practically every reef and affects most coral species in the Caribbean.

IMPACT: Boulder Brain Coral is occasionally killed by parrotfish grazing; however, most stony coral species slowly heal from fish bite injuries.

A terminal phase Stoplight Parrotfish takes a focused bite from a living Lobed Star Coral. Note evidence of repeated biting on adjacent lobes. [right]

Boulder Brain Coral damage from repeated parrotfish bites. [below left]

Longsnout Butterflyfish feeding on Symmetrical Brain Coral; note damage to ridge tops. [below right]

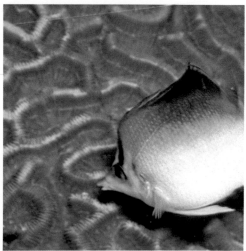

Damselfish Predation

VISUAL ID: Damselfishes, primarily the Threespot, *Stegastes planifrons,* are aggressive, territorial fishes that create algal gardens which they vigorously defended from other herbivores. They typically take numerous small bites over the surface of the coral colony killing an area of living polyps that is colonized by tufts of algae. [right] These injuries have been misidentified as an infection and inappropriately called "White Spot Disease."

Staghorn Coral, *Acropora cervicornis,* and Elkhorn Coral, *A. palmata,* colonies will attempt to grow over the injury, but the damselfish will continue to bite at the same spot causing the production of a chimney-like structure with an algal tuft growing on the end. [far right] Typically, the fish removes many polyps forming numerous chimneys on a single colony. If the damselfish leaves the area, coral tissue will eventually cover the injury creating what appears to be a spire extending from the branch's surface.

Damselfishes tend to damage the projecting ridges of brain corals. As algae colonize the ridges, the fish continue to remove adjacent tissue causing a progressive spread of the algal patch [middle left]. These injuries have also been misidentified as a disease called "Ridge Mortality." *Stegastes planifrons* and *M. chrysurus* will also repeatedly bite at individual lesions on Elkhorn Coral, *A. palmata,* causing them to expand in size in an irregular manner, in a pattern similar to that described for white patch disease (white pox and patchy necrosis). Lesions are often associated with abraded corallites, which is also reported for white pox.

ABUNDANCE & DISTRIBUTION: Damselfish predation occurs throughout the region.

IMPACT: Continued tissue removal by Damselfish can eventually kill an entire colony.

Sponge and Tunicate Overgrowth

Overgrowth and encrustation by organisms competing for space with corals, such as sponges, algae and tunicates, may eventually cause the death of stony corals and gorgonians. Most sponges associated with coral overgrowth first colonize dead areas at the margins of living tissue, or substrate adjacent to colonies. However, some sponge species bore directly into a coral's skeleton by secreting tiny amounts of acid, which riddle the structure with chambers. This damage may compromise the structure to a point where sections break away from the colony. Other competitive sponges and tunicates infiltrate corals by injecting compounds that kill the living tissue of stony corals.

In recent years, the occurrence of overgrowths appears to have increased at many locations around the Caribbean. This growing problem may be the result of excess nutrients, bacteria and suspended particles carried into the sea by runoff stimulating the growth of plankton and, in turn, providing additional food for sponges and tunicates.

Sponges

Most sponges that are associated with corals first colonize exposed skeletal areas that lack living tissue, or the reef substrate adjacent to a coral. They invade a colony from its edge, or from an area that died in the past. The Variable Boring Sponge [next] is unusual, in that its larvae settle on the coral's living surface, kill a portion to expose the underlying skeleton, and then bore into its tissue. **Variable Boring Sponge**, *Siphonodictyon coralliphagum,* varies from bright sulfur-yellow to lemon-yellow [bottom left], orange [middle right] and white [bottom right]. The larvae of this species also kills a small portion of coral tissue. In most cases, the majority of the sponge lives within the internal skeleton of the coral with only its excurrent openings (oscula) extending above the surface; however, on occasion large areas of the sponge are visible [bottom left].

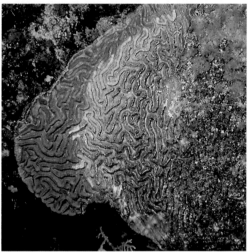

Coral Health and Mortality

Species in genus *Cliona*, which are discussed next, include several species of encrusting sponges that attack and erode the surface of living corals. These sponges kill the living tissue, excavate the upper layers of the coral skeleton, and create a series of cavities and tunnels within the colonies. Members of the genus secrete acid from specialized cells that dissolve, etch and chip away at the coral skeleton and then expel tiny fragments of limestone through the excurrent openings. Because clionid sponges appear to increase in number and size in areas with high concentrations of organic matter and bacteria, their presence may serve in the future as an indicator of pollution.

Red Boring Sponge, *Cliona delitrix,* is bright red-orange. Although the species appears to encrust a coral colony's surface, it actually bores into the limestone skeleton [far right]. Numerous low wart-like spots containing tiny incurrent pores cover the surfaces. Scattered excurrent openings with large fleshy, flexible lips protrude prominently. The sponge attacks mound-building corals and will kill an entire coral colony within several years. Sponge Zoanthid, *Parazoanthus parasiticus,* and Sponge Brittle Star, *Ophiothrix suensonii,* often live on the surface of this species [right].

Coral Encrusting Sponge are two species of identically appearing sponges, *Cliona aprica* and *C. caribea,* that can only be distinguished to species by microscopic examination of their structural spicules. The characteristic brown to olive-brown color is derived from symbiotic algae living within their tissue. Numerous tiny, pore-like excurrent openings cover their smooth surfaces. The sponges rapidly encrust the surfaces of dead coral occasionally covering large portions of a reef's substrate. They later spread over nearly any species of living coral encountered eroding the colonies' to a depth of one half to three quarters of an inch (1 - 2 cm) [right]. A narrow white band of exposed skeleton often separates living coral polyps from the sponge [far right]. Coral polyps bordering the invasion appear undisturbed. The sponge spreads approximately half of an inch (1 cm) a month.

Brown Variable Sponge, *Cliona varians,* forms a soft, thin tan to olive-brown carpet with raised, volcano-shaped excurrent openings that occasionally have irregular raised structures scattered over the surface. These encrustations may be several yards wide. The skeletal features of overgrown corals are often visible beneath the encrustation, but can be distinguished easily by the presence of excurrent openings [right]. The invader kills coral colonies as it spreads [far right]. At least 12 species of corals are known to be affected by Brown Variable Sponge.

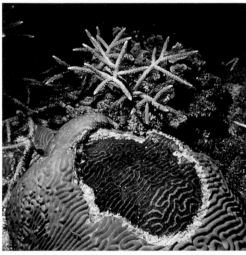

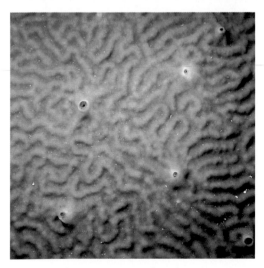

257

Puffy Overgrowing Sponge, *Chondrilla nucula,* is shades of brown with small scattered excurrent openings that protrude above the sponge's surface. Colonies begin on a dead area before spreading over a coral colony's surface killing living tissue as they spread [opposite top right]. The coral's skeletal features are often visible through the encrustation, but the sponge can be differentiated from living coral by its excurrent openings [opposite top left].

Not all encrusting-type sponges overgrow or bioerode living corals. For example, Orange Icing Sponge, *Mycale laevis,* frequently seen underneath the surface of plating corals, actually protects the colony from invading invertebrates [opposite middle left].

Cnidarians

Branching Fire Coral, *Millepora alcicornis,* and **Blade Fire Coral,** *Millepora complanata,* grow in erect colonies in areas with surge or currents [opposite middle right]. On occasion, both species overgrow and encrust neighboring stony corals and gorgonians eventually killing the colonies.

Encrusting Gorgonian, *Erythropodium caribaeorum,* forms a thin mat that often encrusts an area several feet wide [below left & right]. When the polyps' long tentacles are extended, the colony appears fuzzy; when contracted, it has the appearance of smooth brown leather. Colonies usually encrust the sides of reef substrate, but will also overgrow and kill living stony corals.

Encrusting Zoanthid, *Palythoa caribaeorum,* colonies are most abundant in the shallow back reefs and reef crests, where it occurs as mat-like sheets several meters in diameter. It grows unusually fast, at a rate of 2.5 – 4 mm per day. It acquires and dominates space by killing and hindering the growth of its competitors by physical and chemical means. *Palythoa* contains a high molecular weight toxin known as palytoxin. It is capable of overgrowing 22 species of corals.

Encrusting Gorgonian overgrowing colony of Boulder Star Coral.

Encrusting Gorgonian overgrowing colony of Massive Starlet Coral.

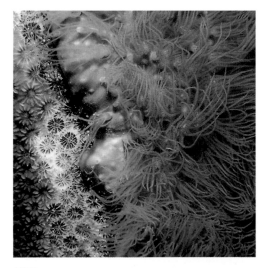

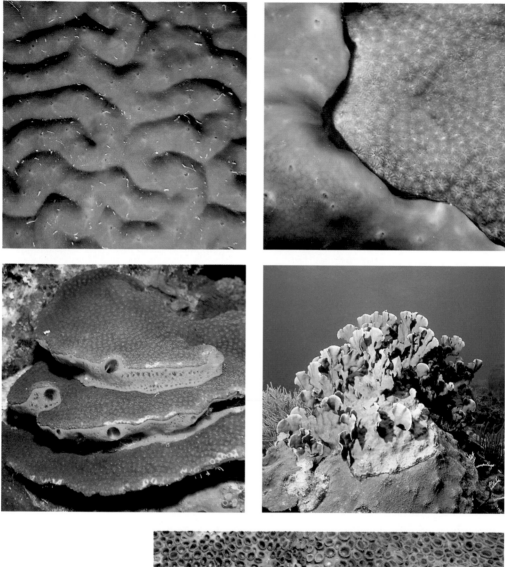

Mat-like sheet of Encrusting Zoanthid overgrowing a colony of White-valley Maze Coral.

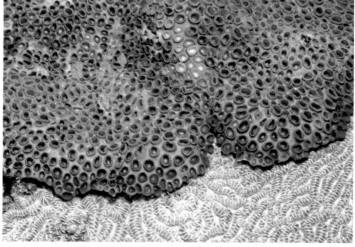

Coral Health and Mortality
Tunicates

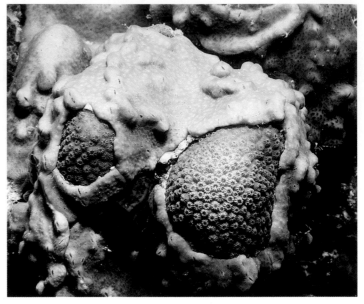

Overgrowing Mat Tunicate, *Trididemnum solidum,* grows in colonies of tiny tunicates embedded in a tough, smooth leathery tunic, which resembles a coating of blue-green or lime-green candle wax. The surface is covered with numerous, pore-like incurrent siphons interspersed with a scattering of larger communal excurrent siphons. Colonies encrust large areas of a reef and will overgrow and kill most species of stony corals. Overgrowing Mat Tunicates often go through periods of rapid growth before dying back, and occasionally disappear completely from an affected area leaving behind exposed substrate. Peeling a colony off a coral is thought to cause further spread of the organism.

Solutions

Coral diseases have probably been around for as long as there have been reefs; however, they are believed to have proliferated due to increasing pressure from an ever-growing human population and stressors associated with climate change. Coral diseases as indicators of environmental deterioration have prompted growing attention from the media, government, non-government agencies, environmental organizations and scientists. The recent losses from disease do appear to have serious long-term ramifications. Coral diseases, at their current levels, often cause coral mortality at rates that greatly exceed the growth of the fastest growing corals. Colonies that are hundreds of years old can be killed by disease in a matter of months, and these corals cannot be replaced in our lifetime. The widespread losses of Elkhorn Coral and Staghorn Coral, two of the three most important reef building corals in the Caribbean, has resulted in major structural changes to reef communities. Because these corals grow relatively quickly, and they can spread through fragmentation, they could show significant recovery within a decade, if conditions improve. The extensive losses of the Lobed, Mountainous and Boulder Star Corals (*Orbicella annularis, O. faveolata* and *O. franski*) from bleaching, white plague and Caribbean Yellow Band Disease over the last decade is more problematic. These species are the dominant frame-building corals of the Caribbean, yet they show very low rates of sexual recruitment and slow growth rates (1 cm/year). Until the mid 1990s, they were dominant in terms of cover and they were the largest corals found on Caribbean reefs. Today, few completely live large colonies remain. Recovery to pre-1995 levels will take centuries under optimal conditions.

In many parts of the Caribbean, losses of live coral may be occurring because reef communities are out of balance. With the dramatic loss of apex predators such as groupers, snappers, barracuda, and other key organisms such as lobsters and octopuses to overfishing, the number of coral eating predators, such as snails, worms and damselfishes have proliferated. Further, depletion

depletion of apex predators has caused increased fishing pressure on herbivores like parrotfishes. Declines in these species may be contributing to phase shifts on reefs toward domination by fleshy algae. The only practical solution for this crisis is a reduction of fishing pressure on key herbivores and other species critical to the health of coral reefs, as well as the restoration of the natural predator/prey relationships through the establishment of a series of Caribbean-wide no-harvest zones.

The Long-spined Urchin, *Diadema antillarum*, an important herbivore that plays a significant role in controlling aggressive growth of fleshy macroalgae, has shown very limited recovery from a mysterious disease that decimated its populations throughout the Caribbean in 1983. In its absence coral reefs have suffered greatly from an explosion of coral-competing macroalgae, which prevents the settlement and survival of coral larvae and also encroaches on established stony corals. It has been documented that coral colonies surrounded by thick algal mats are more susceptible to disease. Recent experiments in Puerto Rico suggest that a reintroduction of sea urchins may reduce Black Band Disease infections.

Limited efforts to treat corals affected by certain diseases have proven highly successful for colonies affected by Blackband Disease. The black bands are aspirated from the colony with a vacuum and the waste material collected to prevent its spread to surrounding corals. Underwater putty is then applied to act as a barrier between the affected area and healthy tissue. This technique has been attempted with some success on colonies with White Band Disease, White Plague and Caribbean Yellow Band Disease with moderate success, but the cost and time required to control disease outbreaks in this manner are unrealistic. Shading colonies affected with Black Band Disease also significantly reduces the disease. Other novel treatments including antibiotics and phage therapy have proven successful for small numbers of infected corals.

While treatments for diseases represent a short-term solution, they can only be conducted on a small scale and are only effective for specific diseases. Region-wide protection of corals from disease organisms will require a more significant effort. Greatly expanded field monitoring to assess the health of coral reefs and additional laboratory studies to better understand the nature of coral diseases are urgently needed.

Another strategy involves the development of restoration technologies to enhance the survival of coral fragments, promote settlement and recruitment of coral larvae, and to culture small branches for eventual reintroduction to degraded areas. Because of the large losses sustained by Elkhorn Coral and Staghorn Coral, NOAA/National Marine Fisheries Service added these species to the Endangered Species Act (ESA) in 2004; a proposal to elevate their status from threatened to endangered, and also list five other species as endangered and two as threatened is under consideration. An ESA listing would prevent harmful activities such as dredging in areas near U.S. coral reefs and provide better protection for the listed corals and the coral reef environment overall. Further, an ESA listing requires the development and implementation of a recovery program in an attempt to restore the species to their former abundance.

Strategies to mitigate land-based threats are paramount for addressing coral diseases. Rivers, coastal run-off and sewage discharge increase the pollutants that enter the coral reef environment, stressing the corals and making them more likely to become diseased. While many people think that run-off and discharge into the ocean are coastal problems, impacts originating far inland have a cumulative effect on the health of coral reefs.

The United Nations Environmental Program's World Conservation Monitoring Center, in collaboration with NOAA/NMFS, established a global coral disease database. This project, which can be viewed at www.coraldisease.org, links coral disease records to existing coral reef maps, and is helping scientists and managers better understand the distribution of diseases and their linkage with human impact. Recreational divers can contribute information to the database using the online data form and the information in this chapter as a tool to assist in the identification of diseases. Your help in identifying locations of disease outbreaks can further help in the development of solutions to mitigate effects associated with the recent emergence of coral diseases.

The Reproduction and Growth of Stony Corals & Gorgonians

To compete successfully in a reef community, corals need to increase both in numbers and in size. Stony corals are notable in the animal kingdom for their complex suite of reproductive strategies both sexual and asexual. Sexual reproduction creates genetically new individuals from the combination of male and female genes produced by different parental colonies. This process is called genetic recombination. Although differences resulting from the shuffling of genes from one generation to the next may be small, the implications can be great over time. New combinations and slight variations over many generations can lead to adaptations that may provide resistance or increased susceptibility to diseases or stresses such as increased temperatures and pollution. Colonies grow larger by adding new polyps through asexual reproduction: the production of genetically identical clones without the union of male and female gametes.

Understanding sexual reproduction of corals is a bit tricky because some coral species have separate male and female colonies whereas other corals are hermaphroditic, producing both eggs and sperm in the same colony. In addition, the fertilization of eggs, which develop into tiny free-living offspring known as **planula larvae,** can take place inside a colony or outside in open water. Corals that develop planula larvae internally are called **brooders;** species that release eggs, sperm or both into the water column are known as **broadcast spawners.**

Most large, reef-building coral species release millions of gametes once a year in precisely synchronized mass-spawning events. Broadcast spawning allows the stationary animals to mix genetically and to disperse offspring over great distances. Such a copious delivery system is also believed to maximize the chances of fertilization and, at the same time, overwhelm predators with more food than they can possibly consume. The exact cues triggering the annual phenomenon remain unclear. The triggering of the spawn is believed to be linked to water temperatures as well as the lunar, tidal and the 24-hour light cycle.

A few broadcast spawners, known as gonochoric species, have separate male and female colonies, and, depending on their sex, either release sperm or eggs, which, with luck, will cross-fertilize somewhere in the vast water column. Most broadcast spawners, however, are hermaphrodites (both sexes occurring in each individual coral polyp). Such polyps once a year package both sperm and eggs into neat little pink gamete bundles that are expelled to the caprice of the currents when a biological clock strikes.

Fertilization, which is possibly aided by sperm attractants, produces planulae larvae that are able to swim on their own by day two. Once in the grasp of tides and currents, the tiny larval coral embarks on a grand voyage that can last for weeks and carry it hundreds of miles from its point of origin. If the speck of life somehow survives the ever-hungry mouths of plankton-picking and filter-feeding invertebrates and fishes, it will one day mysteriously sense to settle on hard substrate in clear shallow water and begin producing a tiny calcium skeleton – the possible genesis of a coral colony that could live for hundreds of years.

In the Caribbean, the magical night of the largest mass coral spawn typically occurs in the evening eight days after the full moon of August when the star coral complex reproduces. If the full moon occurs early in the month, it is possible that a split spawning occurs: the first in August and again in September.

On the night of the mass coral spawn Giant Star Coral, *Montastraea cavernosa,* discharges stream of smoke-like gametes just after dusk; Boulder Star Coral, *Orbicella franksi,* releases egg/sperm bundles around 9:30 p.m.; Lobed Star Coral, *O. annularis* and Mountainous Star Coral, *O. faveolata,* between 10:30 and 11 p.m. Several species of brain corals and *Acropora* (Staghorn and Elkhorn Corals) take place a few days before.

Male Great Star Coral, Montastraea cavernosa, *releasing smoke-like gametes.*

Female Great Star Coral colony releasing gamete bundles.

Maze Coral, Meandrina meandrites, *releasing smoke-like gametes.*

Coral Reproduction

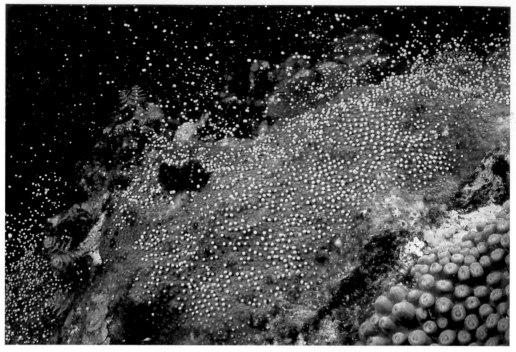

Boulder Star Coral, Orbicella franksi, *releasing gamete bundles.*

Boulder Star Coral, Orbicella franksi, *polyps swollen with gamete bundles.*

Lobed Star Coral, Orbicella annularis, *releasing gamete bundles.*

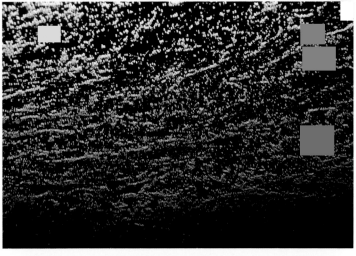

Gamete bundles floating on the surface.

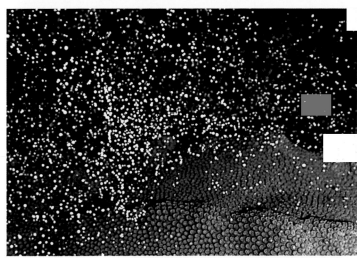

Boulder Star Coral, Orbicella franski, *releasing cloud of gamete bundles.*

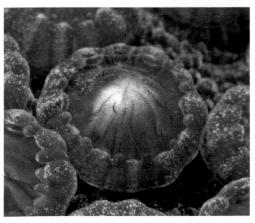

Lobed Star Coral, Orbicella annularis, *polyp swollen with gamete bundle.*

Coral Reproduction

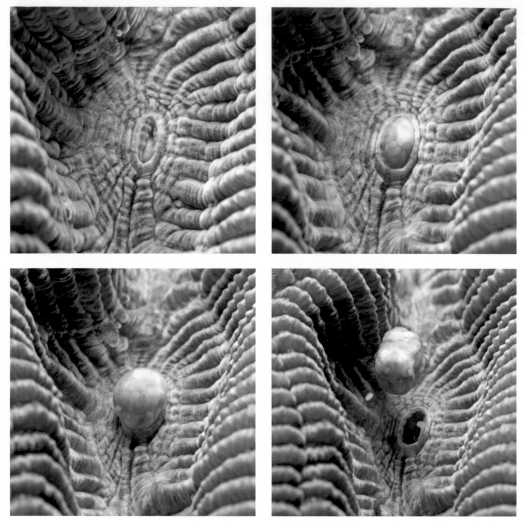

Release of consolidated gamete bundle formed by numerous tiny individual packets. [above]

Polyps of Smooth Flower Coral, *Eusmilia fastigiata*, gathering gamete bundles inside tentacles during the early evening prior to release.
[right]

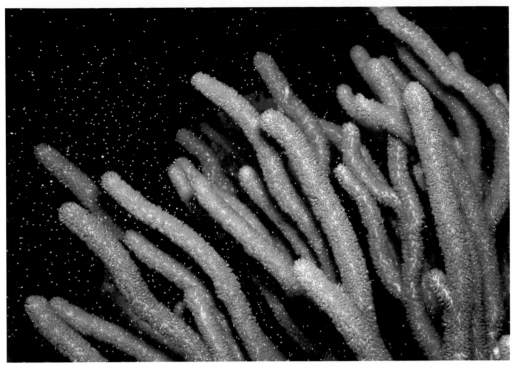

Porous Sea Rod, Pseudoplexaura *sp. releasing tiny gamete bundles in the early evening.* [above]

Close up of Porous Sea Rod releasing gamete bundles. [above & left]

Coral Reproduction

Planula larvae can remain viable for weeks or months while riding the currents in the open water. Soon after settling to the sea floor the specks of life begin secreting a calcium carbonate covering. Soon they are ready to produce new polyps through asexual reproduction—the first step in becoming a colony. New polyps, depending on the species of coral, either erupt between or "bud" from established polyps, a process called extra-tentacular **budding** (literally, outside tentacles), or, as the polyp grows, it divides or splits-off one or more new polyps, a process called **fission** (intra-tentacular budding).

Most of the Caribbean's branching and mound-building corals add new corallites through budding. If closely observed, new smaller corallites can be seen emerging from the base of established corallites on branching corals and erupting between older corallites on the surface mound-building colonies.

Orange Solitary Coral budding a new polyp from the base of the corallite. [below left]
Massive Starlet Coral polyps construct pit-like corallites. The tiny pits between larger corallites are new polyps erupting. [below right]
Tube Coral buds numerous tiny new polyps around larger established corallites. [bottom left]
Staghorn Coral increases the length of branches by budding tiny terminal polyps around their bases. [bottom right]

Coral Reproduction

Brain corals, cactus corals, sheet corals and others that have polyps associated with ridges or grooves generally add new polyps through **fission**. Polyps anywhere along a ridge can replicate in this manner, providing great variation in a colony's shape or ridge pattern. This process can be easily observed in Spiny Flower Coral, *Mussa angulosa*, and Elliptical Star Coral, *Dichocoenia stokesii*.

Large polyp of Spiny Flower Coral divides and splits off three new polyps. [below left]

Smooth Flower Coral polyps dividing into two polyps. [below right]

Knobby Cactus Coral polyp dividing into two polyps. [bottom left]

Golfball Coral polyps lengthen and then fold inward to divide into two polyps; note the long oval corallite starting to fold inward and the two small side-by-side recently divided polyps. [bottom right]

Coral Reproduction

New coral colonies also form by **fragmentation** when pieces of colonies break off due to strong currents, storms, anchor damage, boat grounding, careless divers, or as the result of bio-erosions or predators. If the fragments are of sufficient size and settle on appropriate substrate, they establish distinct new colonies that are genetically identical to the parental colonies. Numerous Caribbean corals are known to reproduce by fragmentation, including branching and pillar and many of the mound-building and boulder corals. It is likely that fragmentation is an important mode of colony replication for many other species.

The advantages of fragmentation over sexual reproduction include increased recruitment rates and likelihood of success, as well as increased abundance and distribution of species in the reef area. A potential disadvantage is minimized genetic diversity. Clonemates will have the same susceptibility to disease or bleaching events, increasing the chance that large numbers of colonies will be affected by adverse conditions.

Broken pieces of Staghorn Coral begin attachment to hard substrate and start upward branching growth regenerating new colonies. Fragmentation is this species' primary means of new colony formation. [below]
Pillar Coral columns, probably broken of by the force of large storm waves, regenerate new colonies. [bottom]

COMMON NAME INDEX

SCIENTIFIC NAME INDEX

NOTES

NOTES